The List Poem

The List Poem

A Guide to Teaching & Writing Catalog Verse

by

Larry Fagin

Teachers & Writers Collaborative
New York, N.Y.

The List Poem

Teachers & Writers Collaborative
5 Union Square West
New York, NY 10003

Library of Congress Cataloging in Publication Data

Fagin, Larry.
     The list poem : a guide to teaching & writing catalog verse / by Larry
Fagin.
           p.   cm.
     Includes bibliographical references.
     ISBN 0-915924-37-4
     1. Poetry—Study and teaching (Elementary)—United States.
    2. Poetry—Study and teaching (Secondary)—United States.
    I. Title
    LB1576.F28   1991
    808.1'071'273—dc20   91-15320
                                                            CIP

Printed by Philmark Lithographics, New York, N.Y.

TABLE OF CONTENTS

Permissions

Acknowledgments

Ideas for this volume germinated at the 1989 Arts Propel Poetry Review Sessions, Princeton, N.J., in conversations with William Bryant Logan, Julie Patton, Nancy Larson Shapiro, JoAnn Doran, Jean Kabbert, Arla Muha, Mary Cunningham Wyse, Rieneke Zessoules, Roberta Camp, Drew Gitomer, and Kristin Powell. Nancy Larson Shapiro encouraged me to write the book. Ron Padgett steered me through it all the way. The following people made valuable suggestions and helped keep my head on straight: Christian McEwen, Susan Noel, Jack Collom, Bob Hershon, Chris Edgar, Elizabeth Fox, Gary Lenhart, Felice Stadler, Jessica Sager, Michael Friedman, Simon Kilmurry, and Steve Levine. Thank you one and all.

•

Teachers & Writers Collaborative is grateful to the following foundations and corporations for their support of its program: American Stock Exchange, Mr. Bingham's Trust for Charity, Louis Calder Foundation, Chemical Bank, Consolidated Edison, DeWitt Wallace-Reader's Digest Fund, Aaron Diamond Foundation, Joelson Foundation, Manufacturers Hanover Trust Company, Morgan Stanley Foundation, New York Rotary Foundation of the Rotary Club of N.Y., New York Telephone, New York Times Company Foundation, Henry Nias Foundation, Helena Rubinstein Foundation, The Scherman Foundation, and The Steele-Reese Foundation.

Teachers & Writers Collaborative is also grateful for funding from the New York State Council on the Arts and the National Endowment for the Arts.

This book is dedicated to Mrs. Grant, my fifth grade teacher.

Introduction

The ideas in this book came out of my work as poet-in-residence at public schools in New York City and elsewhere around the country over the past twenty years. Certain ideas were recommended by other writers. Sometimes students and teachers initiated variations on the assignments.

But my interest in lists and list poems goes back much further. At age eight or so, I memorized the names of the (forty-eight) states, their capital cities, principal products, and state birds and flowers. I skipped the state mottoes (the Latin threw me off). Then I started in on foreign countries. Later, through my reprobate grandfather, I became fascinated with horse racing. Once in a while, the old man would let me place a bet. I remember scanning long lists of the enigmatic names of horses, looking for a likely winner. I even kept track (pardon the pun) of the jockeys—Longden, Arcaro, et al. These are some of my qualifications for authoring this volume.

The list poem (sometimes called "catalog verse") is an excellent way to introduce children, from kindergarten through twelfth grade, to the writing of poetry. It allows one to develop a heightened awareness of the creative process: details (exactness of observation and language), variety, variation, surprise, action, imagery, patterns of sound and rhythm, continuity and repetition.

Another virtue of the list poem is its usefulness in teaching beginners how to write in poetic lines. In list poems, the line is *natural*, because when children write lists, they automatically make line breaks. Later, the teacher can show how to break the lines differently, for more surprising or exotic effects. Because the lines in a list poem tend to be modular, they are especially good for teaching revision: they can be moved around easily, forming different sequences, creating new versions of the poem.

Children already know about lists before they write their first poems. Schools abound in lists. The familiarity and simplicity of the form encourages students to trust their own judgment and gain confidence as poets.

In fact, most of the examples in this book are by children. For some of my assignments there were no appropriate adult poems to serve as models. Children respond with special enthusiasm to each other's work, and their poems have proven useful and influential in the classroom, especially when read aloud. Some of the poems are excerpted; others are on display in their glorious completeness—warts and all.

The children's poems that were created during my school residencies reflect, in varying degrees, my taste, my tone, and my writing procedures. Other teachers will get different results, depending on their personal approaches to writing.

Many of the poems in this book are funny. Comic aspects develop through satire, cartoonlike exaggeration, puns, alliteration, incongruous juxtaposition, and other surprises. Due to the kids' naïveté, sometimes the humor is unintentional.

In the profusion of ideas, topics, and styles, you'll find some overlapping and what appear to be a few inconsistencies. A writing assignment needn't be followed to the letter. I often encourage teachers to vary or even radically change the writing ideas I present to the students.

General Advice about Teaching Poetry Writing

Classroom mood or tone is especially important in learning to write poetry. I try to establish an easy-going but orderly ambience—congenial, with a sense of shared fun and excitement. Grades, competition, and favoritism are counterproductive; they foster inhibition, anxiety, jealousy, and egotism.

Children should write every day, preferably at a specific time, but without a sense of urgency that the work must be completed by the end of the period; it can be continued or finished on another day. Have plenty of paper and pencils on hand. A typewriter or word processor can be useful and exciting. So can a cassette recorder for composing orally and for taping readings, especially in K–3. Teachers should write along with the kids. You who do not consider yourselves to be good writers, why not give it a try? After all, if the kids can do it . . . and your kids will be impressed and inspired by your participation.

Catalog verse draws on specific details of everyday experience, uses rhythms and patterns of common speech, and employs theme and variation to create order and surprise. Images from one's own neighborhood or a list of details about a pet are good starting points for a list poem. At times, the downside of experience intrudes; some writers decide to include painful images of loss or disappointment, and even scenes of inner-city violence, guns, and drugs. Of course, children also write well when fantasizing or using artificial language. A catalog poem of imaginary beings might be a good way to begin writing poetry. Or why not mix reality and fantasy? It's alright for facts to be distorted or exaggerated, associations fanciful or wild.

A brief note about censorship. When kids use "dirty words" in their poems, it's usually pretty silly and a means of getting attention. I try not to make a big deal about it and allow most things to stand in the first draft. They often disappear by the end of the revision.

These days, children "grow up" faster than they used to. Many of them think they want to be in show business. They mimic television, especially adult irony. One fifth grader does a pretty good Henny Youngman imitation: "My third eye can see me trading in my wife for a blonde . . ." These inappropriate references can seem cute at first, but they're not as fresh as the kids' original perceptions.

Children are seduced by the popular images and characters directed at them by television, and often use them in their writing. When the now ubiquitous Bart Simpson or Teenage Mutant Ninja Turtles appear in kids' poems, a tiresome predictability sets in. The kids merely reproduce situations and dialogue they've already seen and heard, without much adaptation. Of course, they don't need these appropriations to write good poetry, as our examples will show.

Warming Up

Start with a theme or topic for the poem, which can be solicited from the children (unless the class is doing "free writing"—no particular form or subject). It can relate to a study topic (whales, outer space, China, black history, the desert), a current event, an imminent holiday, a feeling, or any of the ideas in this book. Whenever possible, I use model poems in class, including many of the examples presented here. Read appropriate examples by adults and children. Point out whatever characteristics you notice: sound and image patterns, surprise, dramatic intensity, simile, etc., but don't overdiscuss or overanalyze them.

Brainstorming

Ask the kids for words, images, phrases, or sentences that relate to the theme. Write them on the board and have everyone copy them on "brainstorm" or scratch sheets. Encourage the children to add to the list on their own. (Certain confident writers prefer to develop the entire list by themselves, or even skip the brainstorming step entirely and go right to the draft.) Emphasize details—specific nouns, interesting or offbeat adjectives, vivid action verbs. (Kids often fall back on weak, bland verbs.) You might give a minilesson on the general versus the specific. For instance, instead of *a man*, why not go for *a short, fat, mean, old, asthmatic, Australian electrician*? Of course, this advice applies to teaching all kinds of writing.

Here's a typical example of a fifth grade brainstorm list for a Halloween poem (see also the brainstorm list for "Night" in chapter 7):

trick or treat	dripping	dungeon
chilling	chains rattling	cellar
ghoul	moans	bats
Frankenstein	screeeeeech!	mice
Dracula	eeeek!!	monsters
ghost	living dead	trembling
mummy	darkness	teeth chattering
skeleton	pitch black	hair standing up
orange & black	rotten eggs	crawling
black cat	candy corn	creepy
full moon	masks	ancient
blood	costumes	cemetery
green skin	red eyes	graveyard
rats	closet	clammy

Draft

With their trusty brainstorm sheets by their sides, the writers are ready for their first drafts. I usually work with the whole class on a beginning. We choose something from the brainstorm list and, together, we develop the first couple of lines. Then the kids continue it individually or begin their own poems. The beginning of a poem can be difficult to write. Kids start slowly, as a rule. The few fearless ones will dive right in and compose a dozen or so dull or awful lines before the poem declares itself and really gets started. The drafts should be spontaneous, written quickly, from the heart (or off the top of the head), legible but sloppy! Far too many children are pathological about neatness, spelling, and punctuation: when they "mess up" they crumple their papers and start over again. Show your students how to cross out lightly (see below), instead of erasing or using dreadful white-out.

The writer needn't try to include all of the words and phrases on the brainstorm sheet. Order and sequence is unimportant in the first draft; the students can juxtapose lines or fragments in the revision. Show them how to double-space the drafts to provide room for future changes. For additions or insertions, demonstrate the use of the caret mark. Here is a draft of a Halloween poem by one of the fifth graders:

> monster
> The ∧ children ~~in their batman costumes~~ play trick or treat and egg the
> windows
>
> Frankenstein comes out of his grave and said "I could of had a
> v-8!"
>
> Bats screech and fly black cats meow
>
> Mummies moan ~~cry help me~~
>
> Dracula says "I vant to suck your blood"
> green   greasy
> ∧ Ghosts in ∧ sheets yell get out of my house!
>   dark
> The graves in the cemetery open up and spirits fly into the ∧ woods
>
> The full moon shines in the sky
>
> Mice run over my feet
>
> I stand and scream wearing my pajamas my hair is standing up
>
> HALLOWEEN MADNESS by Robert Breathard

Notice that our poet has made a good number of changes even before the revision stage. He has added some colorful adjectives and eliminated a couple of phrases. Robert crossed out "in their batman costumes" because a neighbor had, allegedly, copied it from his draft; instead of arguing with the plagiarist, Robert simply dropped his original phrase. For some reason, he tacked on a not very original working title at the end.

Revision

If first drafts are written from the heart, they are revised with the head. Sometimes no revision is needed, but that is rare. Still, it's a good idea to preserve our original impulses in the draft—often we realize that we were right in the first instance—which is why we cross out our "mistakes" *lightly*, just in case. Revision consists of important additions, subtractions, substitutions, and juxtapositions. The writer can sharpen images, strengthen verbs, eliminate redundancy, and impose specificity, clarity, and order. The sequence of the lines can be changed or entire lines can be removed (for instance by lopping off an awkward beginning or ending). It's possible a few minor revisions will alter the mood of a whole poem.

When the kids show you their drafts and revisions, be positive. Negative criticism by the teacher, and especially by one's classmates, is usually a delicate matter, because young writers' feelings about their initial efforts can be fragile. The idea is to improve on a brave beginning, to add clarity, excitement, beauty, surprise, flavor, embellishment.

And now for Robert Breathard's poem, revised:

Let the Red Eyes Shine

Children of monsters play trick or treat and egg the windows of the
    living dead
Frankenstein rises from his grave, screaming "I could of had a V-8!"
Bats screech and mummies moan
Dracula drools, "I vant to suck your blood!"
Green ghosts in greasy sheets drag their chains across the attic floor
The graves in the old cemetery pop open
And the spirits of our ancestors fly into the creepy forest
The full moon glows

I stand in my striped pajamas screaming
My hair is sticking straight up
Mice scamper over my bare toes
Let the red eyes shine!

Quite an improvement! It's a real catalog poem now, not merely a loose assemblage of related images. There's more cohesiveness, much sharper detail, better sound and rhythm, some playfulness, better dramatization, and a touch of genuine scariness at the end (though the title robs the last line of some of its weird intensity).

For starters, there's a crucial switch from "monster children" to "children of monsters," which makes some kind of statement about parents! The "living dead" is a nice addition; I guess they're too catatonic to hand out treats, so they get their windows egged. Frankenstein "rises," (more vivid than the earlier "comes out") to "scream" (not just "say") his funny bit. Robert splices the bats and mummies together in a nifty rhythm, and drops the cliché black cats. Then Dracula "drools" about his thirst. Next, the poet has his ghosts *do* something specific in a specific place. Splitting the seventh line of the first draft in two lends dramatic emphasis. Graves "pop open" rather than merely "open up," the spirits are identified, and "dark woods" changes to the even more ominous "creepy forest" (where all kinds of creatures may be creeping). The moon floats eerily; Robert has wisely deleted the obvious "in the sky;" "glows" is more evocative than "shines." Then he defers the mice until the penultimate line, and he smooths out the awkward run-on sentence of the draft's last line. The reader can really *see* the kid frozen in hysteria; "striped" is a nice touch for the pajamas; "scamper" and "bare toes" are fine improvements on "run" and "feet." Nice going, Robert!

Editorial Polish

Now is the time—not sooner—for corrections in grammar, spelling, and punctuation, to be followed by a final copy, neatly written, typed, or printed out, sometimes with illustrations. There's still a chance for last-minute revisions. (Robert, change that title.) Sometimes, when kids see typed or printed versions of their work, they barely recognize it as theirs—it can be a pleasant shock.

Keep in mind that it's not always necessary to follow the above steps. Variations in the process—or discarding it entirely—may be just as fruitful. Likewise, list poems can be written as prose or as poetry, the only difference being that in the latter form the items in the list can be seen more easily and read aloud more slowly.

Collaboration

Many of the poems in this book are collaborative efforts—most often by small groups or an entire class. One advantage of a group poem is that it allows the children to create something that one writer could not have created alone. Collaboration often yields new ideas and styles that surprise the writers, as well as their readers.

Collaborative writing breaks down our conventional notions of "self-expression," loosens up expectations of a sequential narrative or catalog, and helps the individual writer overcome the desire for absolute control, thereby admitting an unexpected element or "voice" into the creative process. In a collaborative work, the necessary interruptions of any one thought pattern or writing style help young writers realize that in writing they aren't always limited to sounding only like themselves. One poet's lines, phrases, or images is inspired by another's. The poem seems to generate itself spontaneously, rather than reflect one viewpoint or mode of writing. In a sense, the poem itself takes over.

Another advantage of collaboration is that it's extroverted. Students who lack confidence and resist writing at all can be coaxed out of their reluctance when participating in a group effort. They get caught up in the collective excitement and flow of images.

Children working in pairs, passing the paper back and forth, enjoy the give and take of friendly banter. They inspire each other and elaborate on each other's ideas.

When the teacher (or visiting writer) orchestrates collaborations by an entire class, the results can be exciting and unpredictable. This kind of large group work can be accomplished orally, with the teacher or a student taking dictation. (A cassette recorder can come in handy here.) Later, the teacher can also create a collage of individual kids' best or favorite (written) lines, acting as editor-collaborator.

A small group—six or so kids—working closely together over a block of time (more than one period) can produce list poems of great intensity and variety. What follows is an example of just such an experience.

Not long ago I worked with a small, pullout group of talented fifth graders at P.S. 31 in the Bronx. We met nine times. Two terrific poems came out of four meetings toward the middle and end of the residency, one of which, "The Beautiful Poem," was a list poem.

All the children were bright, but one, Steven Figueroa, was particularly loquacious and imaginative—he had adult, sophisticated frames of reference, and he came up with a lot of urbane phrases and comments, not all of which we used.

The kids dictated the lines to me, but I orchestrated and edited the poem somewhat. Sometimes we disagreed about the direction of the poem, and sometimes I'd give in and let them have their way, partly because I was curious as to how far they would take a particular tack. It was all written spontaneously and quickly, and a lot was thrown out, by me or by the students, on the spot or later. "The Beautiful Poem" was originally much longer than it is in the final version (quoted below).

In the workshop in which "The Beautiful Poem" began, I didn't have any idea that we would be writing about beauty, or about any particular subject. I said to the kids, "Somebody, just begin. Poems can start anywhere."

One kid said, "We should say something beautiful."

"O.K. What's beautiful? What's the most beautiful thing in the world?"

"A dress."

"What dress?"

"The beautiful dresses that ladies wear in the spring" (line 1).

I wrote that down and asked the questions essential to all list poems: "What else? What else is beautiful?"

No answers.

"O.K., let's stick with the dresses. What do they look like?"

"The ones with patterns, you know, with stripes and daisies" (line 2).

"O.K. Now what else is beautiful?"

The kids were timid about getting started. One offered, "Music."

"What kind?"

"Songs."

"What kind of songs?"

"Beautiful songs."

"Where do they come from?"

"From the heart."

I wrote down line 3: "The beautiful songs that come from the heart," and asked for another kind of beautiful music, because by now I could see that the poem was organizing itself around the idea of beauty.

When "lovely" got into it (line 7), I asked, "What are some other words than mean *beautiful*?" We made a list, which we used later in the poem: *gorgeous, lovely, extravagant, elegant*, and so on.

The first suggestion for line 10 began, "Beautiful rain falling down . . ." I pointed out that rain *always* falls, so it's boring to say. "What's a different verb?" "Falling" became "pouring." I also asked for an adjective to describe the rain. Among the suggestions, "white" seemed the most inspired. (I don't think the student knew about White Rain shampoo.)

As we went along, a couple of kids began to catch on to the fact that I wanted stronger verbs and more descriptive adjectives: "Glorious birds soaring . . ." But this takes a lot of work. If teachers emphasized a more vivid vocabulary and used it every day in their lessons, the students would start picking it up on their own, and we'd see a dramatic improvement in their writing.

The "beautiful worms" (line 11) must have led to the ground and the flower bed (line 12). One student, Arnulfo Batista, a third grader, came up with the next line (13), which introduced rhyme and a rhetorical inversion new to the workshop writing. I thought that rhyme might then invade the poem, but it didn't, although it did pop up nicely from time to time, as in lines 16–17. Steven Figueroa suggested, for line 17, "Mothers are happy after you've kissed them." I took a hint from Arnulfo's line (13) and supplied the inversion "Happy are mothers . . ."

I'm not sure how we got the idea of line 19, "Going up in the elevator." I think it happened this way: it started with the gold (line 20), a mountain of gold, a beautiful mountain of gold, and when I asked how we'd get to the top, someone said, "By going up in the elevator!" So we worked backwards from line 20 to line 19. I think I moved line 18 up to its present position—originally it was just before "Stay in line" (line 21), which one of the kids kept repeating to me. Only later did I realize that he was referring to my handwriting, which was wandering all over the sheet. "Stay in line" suggested "Everybody stick together," hall monitor talk, or maybe the advice of a nature guide in an adventure story.

Rhyme came back in lines 21–22, with "line" and "shoe-shine," and the nicely polished shoes yielded the idea of something reflected in them. The tininess of the image suggested other small things (lines 23–25).

Somehow this led to things that women use to beautify themselves, and to the sky and birds. The kids saw now that any common thing, like a Barbie doll, could be seen as beautiful, so long as you described it well.

At several points in the writing, someone objected by saying, "But that doesn't make sense." So we talked about what did or didn't make sense, and what that meant, "to make sense." I welcomed criticism as we wrote, but I didn't let the talk degenerate into a gab session that would turn the kids away from their energy for writing. Each time, after maybe a minute I'd get everyone back to the poem.

The first draft turned out to be a catalog about beauty, with brief digressions and narrative moments. The result is fast, free, and full of gorgeous surprises.

The next step was to type up the poem and give the kids copies for us to revise together. Here is our final version:

The Beautiful Poem

The beautiful dresses that ladies wear in the spring
With patterns of stripes and daisies
The beautiful songs that come from the heart
In church soft music blessing Jesus
5   Beautiful toot from toy trumpet
Music of beautiful party people
Lovely sparkling punch
Beautiful conversations in quiet tones of adorable friends and
      family
Hot music of fast dancing
10   Beautiful white rain pouring down on beautiful blue iron roofs
Glorious birds soaring in the trees with pieces of fruit and
      beautiful worms
Flowers wake up, get out of bed
Yellow tulips, roses red

Gorgeous rainbows looping over the clouds
15 Cute toys—bright transformers click and squeak
Hearts are so lovely I can't resist them
Happy are mothers after you've kissed them
Everybody stick together
Going up in the elevator
20 Into the beautiful mountain of gold
Stay in line
Beautiful shoeshine, shoes reflect your image
Small things are beautiful—hamsters, hamburgers
Tinier still—jewelry and coins, butterflies, ladybugs, dominoes,
    string, clover and candy, erasers and baseballs
25 Snowflakes vanishing in a twinkle
Beautiful lipstick applied on lips
Blush and shadow
Powder and perfume
Make women look like Egyptian princesses
30 Make men flip like hot Mexican jumping beans
Pretty sky
Pretty plane
Swans and flamingoes walking on the water
Long sticky legs stirring and paddling
35 Dolls, angelfish, woodpeckers, tweety birds
The beauty of Barbie and her gigantic wardrobe
She flies by in her Porsche with her lovely Ken
Heartbreaking beauty of the death of innocent kittens
Newborn beauty of sunny chicks
40 Beauty of Paris—in bridges and pools
The glory of the Eiffel Tower shaped like an A
Delicate accents of French and Italian like bubbles and flutes
Beautiful sleep
Pleasant dreams
45 Of marriage and kids and love and respect
Beautiful basketball dunked through the hoop
Beautiful school team, beautiful group
Beautiful teacher who cares for us all
Beautiful textbooks, beautiful fall
50 The bell rings
School is out
I run to the candy store
Glamorous licorice, Hershey's, and gum
Extravagant Skittles, cherry and plum

55 Delicious Starburst and 3 Musketeers
   Nestle's Crunch and Baby Ruth
   Beautiful eyeballs
   Beauty of tooth
   Under my pillow
60 The beautiful fairy leaves $10
   My beautiful rich grandfather
   Who gave me an antique
   It's one of a kind
   Uniquely designed
65 An ancient green porcelain Chinese flowerpot
   Its color is lime
   It's cold to the fingers
   Beautiful time . . . running out for this poem
   Beautiful poem
70 Beautiful afternoon—misty sky
   What'll we do now
   The beautiful composition
   The beautiful end

—Rebecca Rosada, Ruben Bermudez, Arnulfo Batista, Steven Figueroa, Michele LaSalle, Zulma Alicea, Marcus Guyton, Melissa Caldero, and José Maldonado

•

With a group of bright students like these, I become quite excited myself. As editor-orchestrator I am right in the thick of it with them. We write the poem together. I'm not the impassive scribe who accepts it all, good and bad. Teacher participation lends intensity to the whole process, and it puts a premium on performance, because no one can hide in such a relatively small group. Of course, not everyone performs well under these circumstances, and some kids are less spontaneous than others. The tactful guide will see to it that no one suffers from the experience.

The next step is to break the group up into say, pairs, and have them work on such poems without my direction or interference. Gradually the kids will find it easier to write alone silently. Sometimes it takes a while for them to internalize what they've experienced in the workshop sessions.

Chapter 1

Historical Background

Lists and catalogs are among the oldest written documents and occur in the literature of most cultures. The desire of the ancients to classify and memorize all of the world's contents in order to gain full knowledge culminated in the great library at Alexandria. Originally, catalog verse was partly a means of providing information or education. Lists of islands and other locations appear in Polynesian and Abyssinian literature. The Phoenicians, among other cultures, inventoried facts and possessions to show the vastness of a battle or the power of a prince. Rhymed catalog verse often outlined conduct for youth. Lists appear throughout the Bible, as in the genealogy of the tribes in Genesis 10.

Book 2 of Homer's *Iliad* includes a long list of ships' captains and their lands of origin. In the *Aeniad* (Book VII), Virgil recalls the many names of kings whose armies "filled the plains" of the Trojan war. Ovid catalogs trees in *Metamorphosis*. In secular medieval poetry, beautiful women are enumerated, and the *blazon*—a list of the beloved's attributes—first appears. Wolfram von Eschenbach included a list of jewels in his medieval romance, *Parzival*, simply because he liked the sound of the words. François Rabelais's *Gargantua and Pantagruel* abounds with lists. In a recent article on this sixteenth-century classic, Geoffrey O'Brien points out Rabelais's obsession with cataloging:

> [. . .] 217 games that Gargantua played as a child, 253 types of food offered up to Master Belly on the island of the Belly-Worshippers, 70 varieties of weapons and armour, 38 healthful effects derived from a "fine green sauce" made from green wheat. These flights of enumeration are not pedantic but expansive. He isn't sealing off new possibilities but demonstrating that there's always more where those came from. Abundance in itself indicates vitality, even if it's abundance of diseases or deformities. The whole material world begs to be classified.

The list appears occasionally in Elizabethan verse. The Earl of

Surrey (ca. 1517–1547) offers a catalog of what one would need to
be happy:

The Happy Life

Martial, the things that do attain
The happy life be these, I find:
The riches left, not got with pain;
The fruitful ground, the quiet mind:

The equal friend, no grudge nor strife;
No charge of rule nor governance;
Without disease, the healthful life;
The household of continuance:

The mean diet, no delicate fare;
True wisdom join'd with simpleness;
The night dischargéd of all care,
Where wine and wit may not oppress:

The faithful wife, without debate;
Such sleeps as may beguile the night:
Contented with thine own estate
Ne wish for death, ne fear his might.

Robert Herrick (1591–1674) composed an inventory of his
poetic subjects, a kind of table of contents in closed couplets:

The Argument of His Book

I sing of brooks, of blossoms, birds, and bowers:
Of April, May, of June, and July-flowers.
I sing of may-poles, hock-carts, wassails, wakes,
Of bride-gowns, brides, and of their bridal-cakes.
I write of youth, of love, and have access
By these, to sing of cleanly-wantonness.
I sing of dews, of rains, and piece by piece
Of balm, of oil, of spice and ambergris.
I sing of times trans-shifting; and I write
How roses first came red, and lilies white.
I write of groves, of twilights, and I sing

The court of Mab, and of the Fairie-King.
I write of hell; I sing (and ever shall)
Of heaven, and hope to have it after all.

John Milton (1608–1674) describes an entire council of fallen angels in *Paradise Lost* (Book II). William Blake (1757–1827) used a partial catalog in his poem "Jerusalem" and in other poems.

One of the most delightful (and peculiar) catalogs in literature occurs in *Jubilate Agno* by Christopher Smart (1722–1771). This long visionary poem consists of fragments, each of which begins with either "Let" or "For." It is a detailed portrait of his cat Jeoffry:

For I will consider my cat Jeoffry.
For he is the servant of the Living God and daily serving him.
For at first glance of the glory of God in the East he worships in his way.
For is this done by wreathing his body seven times round with elegant
    quickness.
For then he leaps up to catch the musk which is the blessing of God
    upon his prayer.
For he rolls upon prank to work it in.
For having done duty and received blessing he begins to consider
    himself.
For this he performs in ten degrees.
For first he looks upon his fore-paws to see if they are clean.
For secondly he kicks up behind to clear away there.
For thirdly he works it upon stretch with the fore-paws extended.
For fourthly he sharpens his paws by wood.
For fifthly he washes himself.
For sixthly he rolls upon wash.
For seventhly he fleas himself, that he may not be interrupted upon the
    beat.
For eighthly he rubs himself against a post.
For ninthly he looks up for his instructions.
For tenthly he goes in quest of food.
For having consider'd God and himself he will consider his neighbor.
For if he meets another cat he will kiss her in kindness.
For when he takes his prey he plays with it to give it a chance.
For one mouse in seven escapes by his dallying.
For when his day's work is done his business more properly begins.
For he keeps the Lord's watch in the night against the adversary.
For he counteracts the powers of darkness by his electrical skin &
    glaring eyes.

For he counteracts the Devil, who is death, by brisking about the life.

For in his morning orisons he loves the sun and the sun loves him.

For he is of the tribe of Tiger.

For the Cherub Cat is a term of the Angel Tiger.

For he has the subtlety and hissing of a serpent, which in goodness he
    suppresses.

For he will not do destruction if he is well-fed, neither will he spit
    without provocation.

For he purrs in thankfulness, when God tells him he's a good cat.

For he is an instrument for the children to learn benevolence upon.

For every house is incomplete without him & a blessing is lacking in
    the spirit.

For the lord commanded Moses concerning the cats at the departure
    of the Children of Israel from Egypt.

For every family had one cat at least in the bag.

For the English cats are the best in Europe.

For he is the cleanest in the use of his fore-paws of any quadruped.

For the dexterity of his defence is an instance of the love of God to him
    exceedingly.

For he is the quickest to his mark of any creature.

For he is tenacious of his point.

For he is a mixture of gravity and waggery.

For he knows God is his Savior.

For there is nothing sweeter than his peace when at rest.

For there is nothing brisker than his life when in motion.

For he is of the Lord's poor and so indeed is he called by benevolence
    perpetually—Poor Jeoffry! poor Jeoffry the rat has bit thy throat.

For I bless the name of the Lord Jesus that Jeoffry is better.

For the divine spirit comes about his body to sustain it in complete cat.

For his tongue is exceedingly pure so that it has in purity what it wants
    in music.

For he is docile and can learn certain things.

For he can set up with gravity which is patience upon approbation.

For he can fetch and carry, which is patience in employment.

For he can jump over a stick which is patience upon proof positive.

For he can spraggle upon waggle at the word of command.

For he can jump from an eminence into his master's bosom.

For he can catch the cork and toss it again.

For he is hated by the hypocrite and miser.

For the former is afraid of detection.

For the latter refuses the charge.

For he camels his back to bear the first notion of business.

For he is good to think on, if a man would express himself neatly.
For he made a great figure in Egypt for his signal services.
For he killed the Icneumon-rat very pernicious by land.
For his ears are so acute that they sting again.
For from this proceeds the passing quickness of his attention.
For by stroking of him I have found out electricity.
For I perceived God's light about him both wax and fire.
For the Electrical fire is the spiritual substance, which God sends from
    heaven to sustain the bodies both of man and beast.
For God has blessed him in the variety of his movements.
For, tho he cannot fly, he is an excellent clamberer.
For his motions upon the face of the earth are more than any other
    quadruped.
For he can tread to all the measures upon the music.
For he can swim for life.
For he can creep.

Catalog verse is, of course, not strictly a western form. The
following Navajo supplication is probably derived from an oral
tradition that began long before Europeans arrived in North America.

A Prayer of the Night Chant

Tségihi.
House made of dawn.
House made of evening light.
House made of the dark cloud.
House made of male rain.
House made of dark mist.
House made of female rain.
House made of pollen.
House made of grasshoppers.
Dark cloud is at the door.
The trail out of it is dark cloud.
The zigzag lightning stands high upon it.
Male deity!
Your offering I make.
I have prepared a smoke for you.
Restore my feet for me.
Restore my legs for me.
Restore my body for me.
Restore my mind for me.

This very day take out your spell for me.
Your spell remove for me.
You have taken it away for me.
Far off it has gone.
Happily I recover.
Happily my interior becomes cool.
Happily I go forth.
My interior feeling cool may I walk.
No longer sore, may I walk.
Impervious to pain, may I walk.
With lively feelings may I walk.
As it used to be long ago, may I walk.
Happily may I walk.
Happily, with abundant dark clouds, may I walk.
Happily, with abundant showers, may I walk.
Happily, with abundant plants, may I walk.
Happily, on a trail of pollen, may I walk.
Happily may I walk.
Being as it used to be long ago, may I walk.
May it be beautiful before me.
May it be beautiful behind me.
May it be beautiful below me.
May it be beautiful above me.
May it be beautiful all around me.
In beauty it is finished.

Catalog verse began to change in the nineteenth century. Walt Whitman broadened the spectrum of things and experiences that could be included in list poetry. In his work there is a realization of the interconnectedness of all life's aspects; the individual becomes aware of being at one with the world. (Native Americans realized this too, long before Whitman.) The final section of his "Crossing Brooklyn Ferry" contains a list of dramatic commands that celebrate everything he can see as he crosses the East River:

Flow on, river! flow with the flood-tide, and ebb with the ebb-tide!
Flow on, crested and scallop-edg'd waves!
Gorgeous clouds of the sunset! drench with your splendor me, or the
    men and women generations after me!
Cross from shore to shore, countless crowds of passengers!
Stand up, tall masts of Mannahatta! stand up, beautiful hills of
    Brooklyn!

Throb, baffled and curious brain! throw out questions and answers!
Suspend here and everywhere, eternal float of solution!
Gaze, loving and thirsty eyes, in the house or street or public assembly!
Sound out, voices of young men! loudly and musically call me by my
nighest name!
Live, old life! play the part that looks back on the actor or actress!
Play the old role, the role that is great or small according as one makes
it! [. . .]
Fly on, sea-birds! fly sideways, or wheel in large circles high in the air;
Receive the summer sky, you water, and faithfully hold it till all
downcast eyes have time to take it from you!
Diverge, fine spokes of light, from the shape of my head, or any one's
head, in the sunlit water!
Come on, ships from the lower bay! pass up or down, white-sail'd
schooners, sloops, lighters!
Flaunt away, flags of all nations! be duly lower'd at sunset!
Burn high your fires, foundry chimneys! cast black shadows at nightfall!
cast red and yellow light over the tops of the houses! [. . .]

Randall Jarrell's essay "Some Lines from Whitman" (in *Poetry
and the Age*) takes a close look at how Whitman proceeds with his
panoramic list-making:

Whitman is more coordinate and parallel than anybody, is *the* poet of
parallel present participles, of twenty verbs joined by a single subject:
all this helps to give his work its feeling of raw hypnotic reality, of being
that world which also streams over us joined only by *ands*, until we
supply the subordinating conjunctions; and since as children we see the
ands and not the *becauses*, this method helps to give Whitman some of
the freshness of childhood. How inexhaustibly interesting the world is
to Whitman!

Jarrell goes on:

Very often the things presented form nothing but a list:

The pure contralto sings in the organ loft,
The carpenter dresses his plank, the tongue of his foreplane
whistles its wild ascending lisp,
The married and unmarried children ride home to their
Thanksgiving dinner,

The pilot seizes the king-pin, he heaves down with a strong
   arm,
The mate stands braced in the whale-boat, lance and harpoon
   are ready,
The duck-shooter walks by silent and cautious stretches,
The deacons are ordain'd with cross'd hands at the altar,
The spinning-girl retreats and advances to the hum of the big
   wheel,
The farmer stops by the bars as he walks on a First-day loafe
   and looks at the oats and rye,
The lunatic is carried at last to the asylum a confirm'd case,
(He will never sleep any more as he did in the cot in his
   mother's bed-room;)
The jour printer with gray head and gaunt jaws works at his
   case,
He turns his quid of tobacco while his eyes blur with the
   manuscript,
The malform'd limbs are tied to the surgeon's table,
What is removed drops horribly in a pail; . . .

It is only a list—but what a list! And how delicately, in what different
ways—likeness and opposition and continuation and climax and anti-
climax—the transitions are managed, whenever Whitman wants to
manage them. Notice them in the next quotation, another "mere list":

The bride unrumples her white dress, the minute-hand of the
   clock moves slowly,
The opium-eater reclines with rigid head and just-open'd lips,
The prostitute draggles her shawl, her bonnet bobs on her tipsy
   and pimpled neck . . .

The first line is joined to the third by *unrumples* and *draggles, white dress*
and *shawl*; the second to the third by *rigid head, bobs, tipsy, neck*; the first
to the second by *slowly, just-open'd,* and the slowing-down of time in
both states. And occasionally one of these lists is metamorphosed into
something we have no name for; the man who would call the next
quotation a mere list—anybody will feel this—would boil his babies up
for soap.

Ever the hard unsunk ground,
Ever the eaters and drinkers, ever the upward and downward
   sun,

Ever myself and my neighbors, refreshing, wicked, real,
Ever the old inexplicable query, ever that thorned thumb, that
breath of itches and thirsts,
Ever the vexer's hoot! hoot! till we find where the sly one
hides and bring him forth,
Ever the sobbing liquid of life,
Ever the bandage under the chin, ever the trestles of death.

Since Whitman, lists have been used more prevalently by twentieth-century European poets, especially those influenced by him, such as Valery Larbaud, Federico García Lorca, Fernando Pessoa, and Pablo Neruda.

Allen Ginsberg's poetry has Whitman's inclusiveness and generosity, and something of Whitman's incisiveness. He, too, is a writer of the biblical long line—a tradition typical of American poetics, from Whitman through Edward Carpenter, Vachel Lindsay, Robinson Jeffers, Marsden Hartley, Kenneth Koch, and John Ashbery, and in the expansive prose of Herman Melville, Thomas Wolfe, and Jack Kerouac. Ginsberg's most well-known poems, "Howl" and "Kaddish," are fine examples of long-lined catalog verse, using phrase repetition to create dramatic intensity.

[. . .]
who vanished into nowhere Zen New Jersey leaving a trail of
ambiguous picture postcards of Atlantic City Hall, suffering
Eastern sweats and Tangerian bone-grindings and migraines of
China under junk-withdrawal in Newark's bleak furnished room,
who wandered around and around at midnight in the railroad yard
wondering where to go, and went, leaving no broken hearts,
who lit cigarettes in boxcars boxcars boxcars racketing through snow
toward lonesome farms in grandfather night,
who studied Plotinus Poe St. John of the Cross telepathy and bop
kaballa because the cosmos instinctively vibrated at their feet in
Kansas,
who loned it through the streets of Idaho seeking visionary indian
angels who were visionary indian angels,
who thought they were only mad when Baltimore gleamed in
supernatural ecstasy,
who jumped in limousines with the Chinamen of Oklahoma on the
impulse of winter midnight streetlight smalltown rain,

who lounged hungry and lonesome though Houston seeking jazz or
sex or soup, and followed the brilliant Spaniard to converse about
America and Eternity, a hopeless task, and so took ship to Africa,
who disappeared into the volcanoes of Mexico leaving behind nothing
but the shadow of dungarees and the lava and ash of poetry
scattered in fireplace Chicago [. . .]

(from "Howl")

The inclusiveness of long lines seems to encourage catalogs, but contemporary list poems can be short too, as you will see in some of the examples later in this book.

Chapter 2

This Little Piggy (Lists and List Poems)

The first thing I did in preparing material for this book was to make a list of ideas and arrange them in order of importance. I barely noticed that I was making a list. List-making is such a familiar activity that most of us take it for granted and seldom, if ever, pay attention to the list or catalog as a form in itself. Lists are the stuff of everyday life: shopping lists, stock inventories, rosters and attendance sheets, reminders, telephone and address books, travel itineraries and other schedules, price lists, dictionaries, vocabularies, instructions, tables of contents, indices, bibliographies, card catalogs, mail-order catalogs, recipes, menus, rules and regulations, contest results, top tens, hit parades, best dressed, worst dressed, most wanted, blessings, wish lists, resolutions, deadly sins, commandments, musketeers, dwarfs, seas, winds, Days of Christmas, Horsemen of the Apocalypse, Pillars of Wisdom, Wonders of the World. And there you have it—a list of lists.

Good lists and catalogs are compelling. Witness the popularity of *The Guinness Book of World Records* or *The Book of Lists*. Some lists are personal notes, reminders jotted down randomly on scraps of paper. Other lists are carefully considered, detailed, prioritized, typed or even published, posted or distributed. Most lists are practical, though some people keep lists compulsively, or for no apparent reason. F. Scott Fitzgerald, throughout his life, kept a descriptive list of all the many shoes he owned. P. F. Herman of Hull, England, recorded each time and place he sneezed. Many people keep diaries that note everything they eat. Making lists begins early in childhood. Toddlers learn to keep track of their toes ("This little piggy. . ."), rudimentary counting, and the ABCs. Certain nursery rhymes and songs, such as "The House That Jack Built" or "Old MacDonald Had a Farm," are catalogs of a sort. This rote learning may involve ordering items in sequences and groups, giving the list a particular shape or character.

Having considered the list as a natural form and indicated some of its uses in society, we now come to the list *poem*. What exactly *is* it, you may well ask, and what is the difference between a *list* and a *list poem*? Here are some basic types and functions of the latter:

1) to define a concept, person, or thing (eg., beauty, a teacher, a submarine) by listing its different facets, characteristics, actions, or effects. See chapter 4 (Oxen Should Have Very Small Foreheads) for examples of this type;

2) a listing of things to show progression, generation, or commonality, usually without transitional ideas or phrases (to further compactness and dramatic effect). The *I Remember* poem in chapter 3 (Memories) fits this description well;

3) instruction, prescription, guidance—things to do and how to do them. See chapter 6 (Things to Do) and chapter 9 (How to Behave at a Fancy Party);

4) a display of order and classification; inventories. See the menus in chapter 10 (Menus, Haircuts, Fashion Notes, and Popular Dances) and, in chapter 13 (Grab Bag; *Letters, Lineups,* and the poem "Ten Things I'll Need on a Desert Island" in *Hodgepodge*);

5) chronologies, milestones, history records. (See *Last Day on Earth* in chapter 13.)

As to when or how a list becomes a poem, there are a number of opinions and considerations. A mere shopping list or recipe doesn't necessarily add up to a poem. Something else must happen along the way.

Surprise in the sequence—a poetic bump in the road—is often desirable. The inclusion of something that doesn't belong will appeal to the eye, the imagination, and hopefully a sense of humor:

wolf
bear
ant
turkey
leopard
shoelaces
whale
anteater
skunk
    —*Anonymous*

In the list above, the placement is of vital importance. If *shoelaces* came first it would be anticlimactic; if last, too obvious. A certain amount of build-up (expectation) and release gives the list poem a shape, in which surprise is possible.

A list poem can occasionally *begin* with a surprise: "I am afraid of being trapped in an umbrella." It's often a matter of choosing what to spring on the unsuspecting reader and when to spring it—timing. You'll find many of the poems in this book teeming with unexpected words, images, and even sounds.

Sometimes an odd concept for a sequence can qualify it as a poem. For example, a combination of real and imaginary haircuts or ice-cream flavors, or a litany of elaborate insults are not exactly run-of-the-mill poetic topics. Among other offbeat ideas: Anne Waldman's "Things That Go Away and Come Back," Charles North's "Lineups," David Antin's "Delusions of the Insane," and Paul Simon's song, "Fifty Ways to Leave Your Lover."

Gertrude Stein wrote, "Poetry is loving the name of anything." Names in themselves can have an evocative quality and a list of them can constitute a poem, depending on the treatment—their juxtapositions, sound, rhythm, and certain indefinable associative characteristics. Names of places along a route or on a travel itinerary often stir the imagination. Lists of place names appear commonly in popular and folk music, as well as in poetry. Johnny Mercer's "Atchison, Topeka, and Santa Fe," Bobby Troup's "(Get Your Kicks on) Route 66," and Hank Snow's "I've Been Everywhere," are fine examples of the genre. John Ashbery's poem "Into the Dusk-Charged Air" contains the name of a river in each of its 152 lines. The lines wind and flow like a river:

> [. . .]
> The Rhone slogs along through whitish banks
> And the Rio Grande spins tales of the past.
> The Loire bursts its frozen shackles
> But the Moldau's wet mud ensnares it.
> The East catches the light.
> Near the Escaut the noise of the factories echoes
> And the sinuous Humboldt gurgles wildly.
> The Po too flows, and the many-colored
> Thames. Into the Atlantic Ocean
> Pours the Garonne. Few ships navigate
> On the Housatonic, but quite a few can be seen
> On the Elbe. For centuries

The Afton has flowed.
                    If the Rio Negro
Could abandon its song, and the Magdalena
The jungle flowers, the Tagus
Would still flow serenely, and the Ohio
Abrade its slate banks [. . .]

The following excerpt from Valery Larbaud's "Europe" does not follow such a rigorous plan, but it too has the magic of names:

And you, ports of Istria and Croatia
And the Dalmatian coast, green and grey and pure white!
The bright bay at Pola is full of war-ships
Between banks of green lawns, ships flying
Red and white flags beneath a delicate sky.
Kherso, Abbazzia, Fiume, Veglia, new towns
Or which at least seem new, who
Knows why! Zara, Sebenico, Spalato and Ragusa,
Like a basket of flowers tilted near the waves,
And the Mouths of Cattaro, where
You can follow the sea forever among mountains
Crenelated with inaccessible Venetian citadels.
O Cattaro, little box, little fortress one might give
To a child for Christmas (it even has greenish soldiers stationed at the
     gate),
Building blocks, but filled
With the scent of roses coming from who knows where.
     —*Translated by Ron Padgett and Bill Zavatsky*

Henry Thomas's song "Railroadin' Some" is little more than an itemization of the towns he passes through on a train ride, but it has the joy of travel in it:

Leaving Fort Worth, Texas!
Going through Dallas!
Hello, Terrell!
Grand Saline!
Silver Lake!
Mineola!
Tyler!
Longview!

27

Jefferson!
Marshall!
Little Sandy!
Big Sandy!
Texarkana!
I'm on my way but I don't know where!

It's possible that French poet Paul Morand, traveling in the U.S.
in the 1920s, was influenced by songs such as Thomas's:

Santa Fe Deluxe

This is the Southwest
where Mexican influences make themselves felt in the kinds of horses
    and steeples.
People stick their tickets in the bands of their big felt hats.
The locomotive,
its eye in the middle of its belly,
shines on the track and the crossties,
alternating dark and light, like a keyboard.
Arizona is next to California
like a skinny girl next to a fat woman.
The deluxe Santa Fe Chief
is due at the following times:

Baghdad	5:00
Troy	5:30
Cadiz	5:52
Siam	6:21
Seligman	7:00
Albuquerque	7:12
Gallinas	7:45
Mission	8:01
Levy (breakfast)	8:32
Optimo	8:47
Dumas	9:03
Hamburg	9:28
Syracuse	9:50
Wagner	10:05
Raton	10:17
Marinette	11:00
Hamlet	11:31

    —Translated by Bill Zavatsky and Ron Padgett

On occasion, one runs across a published list—a found item—so strange and exotic that it's like a poem, such as this excerpt from a magic shop catalog:

Electronic Lucky Light
High Sign
Spear-it Knife
Trapezy Ribbon
The Rattle Box
Chapeaugraphy
Melto Ring
Sucker Chinese Paper Tear
The Scotch Purse
Crystal Fire Bowl
French Paddles
Technicolor Thimbles
Glorious Beer
The Crawler
Nest of Alarm Clocks
Fraidy Cat Rabbit
Popsy Pegs
Spotted Milk
Eerie Ribbons
Improved Proxy Substitution Chest
The Appealing Orange Box
Mental Epic
The Goofus Plant (Deluxe)
Invisible Bovine
Rubber Canaries
Flash

The word combinations themselves are magical; and one wonders what all this stuff *does*. Here's a list of titles from a photography exhibit. The individual titles are unremarkable, but in the context of the list, the images and sounds play off each other and create "poetic" effects:

Squad
Beehive
Shaved Head
Assembly

Woodsman
Drum Set
Sword Swallower
Interpreter
Prodigy
Ballroom Couple
Singing Boys
Bouncing Balls
Building Blocks
Diamond
Airmen
Workers

The attraction of these "found poems," other than their strangeness, is in their variety and randomness; they have many unanticipated "bumps in the road." On the other hand, obsessive organization in composing is also fascinating, especially when it goes to extremes. Swiss philosopher Max Picard's *The World of Silence* (see excerpt in chapter 4) obsesses over the word *silence*, which appears in almost every sentence in the book! Of course, catalog verse often takes on a slightly hypnotic or crazed quality through systematic repetition or an accumulation of images and sounds.

Another way for a list to become a poem is through heightened emotion, a cumulative build-up of excitement or excitedness. One thinks of the epic-scale, long-lined poems of Walt Whitman or Allen Ginsberg, but even a simple list can possess this quality. The bone-bare itinerary of Henry Thomas's "Railroadin' Some" becomes charged with emotion—even if one disregards the exclamation points—as his trip continues.

As I mentioned earlier, list poetry can also occur in prose. Rabelais is the first author who comes to mind. Writers as diverse as James Joyce, F. Scott Fitzgerald, Jack Kerouac, and Donald Barthelme delighted in lists of all kinds. John Cheever once said, "You can use an invitation list as a lyrical poem. A sort of evocation." In his story, "The Swimmer," Cheever includes a list of names representing stops on the protagonist's route as he tries to swim across town via his neighbors' swimming pools:

The only maps and charts we had to go by were remembered or imaginary but these were clear enough. First there were the Grahams, the Hammers, the Lears, the Howlands, and the Crosscups. He would cross Ditmar Street to the Bunkers and come, after a short portage, to the Levys, the Welchers, and the public pool in Lancaster. Then there were the Hallorans, the Sachses, the Biswangers, Shirley Adams, the Gilmartins and the Clydes.

Jack Kerouac's books abound in poetic lists of things seen, heard, eaten, or imagined. This is from *Lonesome Traveler:*

I saw that Frisco California white and gray of rain fogs and the back alleys of bottles, breens, derbies, mustachios of beer, oysters, flying seals, crossing hills, bleak bay windows, eye diddle for old churches with handouts for seadogs barkling and snurling in avenues of lost opportunity time, ah—loved it all . . .

There is no absolute way of telling when a list becomes a list poem: it is often a matter of individual perception. Some lists remain just lists, while others "take off."

Chapter 3

Memories

Joe Brainard's *I Remember* is a minor classic, a book-length list of memories, in no particular order, usually averaging a sentence or two each, about growing up in 1950s America. Here is a collaged sampling:

> I remember the only time I ever saw my mother cry. I was eating apricot pie.
> I remember how much I used to stutter.
> I remember the first time I saw television. Lucille Ball was taking ballet lessons.
> I remember Aunt Cleora who lived in Hollywood. Every year for Christmas she sent my brother and me a joint present of one book.
> I remember a very poor boy who had to wear his sister's blouses to school.
> I remember shower curtains with angel fish on them.
> I remember very old people when I was very young. Their houses smelled funny.
> I remember daydreams of being a singer all alone on a big stage with no scenery, just one spotlight on me, singing my heart out, and moving my audience to total tears of love and affection.
> I remember waking up somewhere once and there was a horse staring me in the face.
> I remember saying "thank you" in reply to "thank you" and then the other person doesn't know what to say.
> I remember how embarrassed I was when other children cried.
> I remember one very hot summer day I put ice cubes in my aquarium and all the fish died.
> I remember laundromats at night all lit up with nobody in them.
> I remember opening jars that nobody else could open.
> I remember not understanding why people on the other side of the world didn't fall off.
> I remember winning a Peter Pan Coloring Contest and getting a free pass to the movies for a year.
> I remember bongo drums.

I remember candles in wine bottles.

I remember putting on suntan oil and having the sun go away.

I remember jumping off the front porch head first onto the corner of a brick. I remember being able to see nothing but gushing red blood. This is one of the first things I remember. And I have a scar to prove it.

Here is a topic on which the writer—child or adult—is always a bona fide expert: your own life, what you remember of it. Of course, the ability or talent to remember varies greatly from person to person. Some details are fuzzy; others snap into focus. The classroom atmosphere may induce lucid recollections for certain students and interfere with the process for others. Some of us need to be alone, in a tranquil setting, in order for memory to function efficiently, although reading or listening to the remembrances of friends or classmates will often jog our own memories. Young writers who draw an occasional blank or even suffer from temporary amnesia might turn to Mom or Dad or a family photo album for help in remembering all kinds of things.

I often begin a residency in a school with the "I Remember" assignment. It helps develop a heightened consciousness of details— the particulars of daily life—so important to creative writing. It gives kids a chance to record a kind of autobiography, an overview of their lives. It's also a good way to learn more about the kids and their backgrounds. Finally, it's stimulating for kids to share each other's experiences, to notice how we are simultaneously different and similar. Here are a few examples:

I remember my bird Louie who talked too much.

I remember kissing someone I thought was my mother.

I remember that when I got to my father's house in Mexico I got scared because there were fat animals that looked like monsters. They were called cows.

I remember when my brother was born. He wasn't as ugly as my sister.

I remember spitting in a lady's face at the movies.

I remember eating a roach with sour cream.

I remember when I went to the beach, the blue water.

I drank the salted water.

—*Michael Torres, fifth grade*

I remember they took something out of my throat that I don't remember the name of.

I remember when I was angry with my friend, I didn't speak to her for
a month because I wanted to teach her a lesson. Then, when I tried
to make friends again, she wouldn't speak to me, and we never
were friends again.
I remember there was a broken oven and this boy tried to put me in
there and cook me.
I remember one Christmas a fireman gave me a little moon with a wish
on it.
I remember when I was getting skinny I was very proud of myself.
I remember the most beautiful place in the world: Co-op City.
—*Lakisha Dennis, third grade*

I remember the time I pushed my dog down two flights of stairs and
she came running back to the top and laid on the edge so I could
push her again.
I remember my first set of Weeble Wobbles. I smashed them with a
hammer.
I remember when my brother threw my underwear out the window.
It landed in a tree and the next day we found that a bird had built
its nest in it.
I remember a dream about a blinking cowboy.
I remember when my mother made a blue sock for me.
I remember when my aunt said to take care of Kelly. I said, "What?"
I love my family.
—*Alex Wagner, fourth grade*

I remember when I jumped in a pool and a big turtle popped out.
I remember school lunch. My pizza had two staples in it.
I remember the day my cousin Paul electrocuted his fish. I never
wanted to remember this again.
I remember a very special friend that I don't have any more for no
reason at all.
I remember when I used to see things on my walls at night, like a baby
carriage and raccoons.
—*Alexandra Fein, fourth grade*

One way to organize the *I Remember* assignment is to read a few
good examples and turn the kids loose to record their memories in a
random fashion. Another, more deliberate method is to read examples,
then set up a brainstorm sheet that organizes memories by categories. In
the topics below, I've excerpted lines from longer poems to give

examples related to the particular topic. The single lines provide a good way of looking at the internal workings of list poems.

Earliest (Preschool) Memories. Who remembers their first words or taking their first step? These events are not often remembered but rather are told to us by our parents. They become part of family folklore and are sometimes exaggerated in the telling. I used to swear that I remembered being saved from a burning crib by a fireman, but I was giving a distorted version of what my mother more accurately recalled and passed on to me: she was the "fireman" who put out a small fire in the next room. Oh, well. Some people are blessed with (or burdened by) total recall and claim to remember the day they were born. Who's to say they don't?

> I remember when I was born, seeing all these ugly faces—one smiling with glasses and one that looked like a fish.
> —*Diane Farmaco, fourth grade*

> I remember taking my first step and falling on my rabbit.
> —*Cleo White, fourth grade*

> I remember singing for the first time. It was "That's Amore."
> —*Gina DeLucca, fifth grade*

> I remember when I let bugs crawl up my arms.
> —*Anonymous, third grade*

> I remember jumping into a pool. It wasn't a pool. It was a puddle.
> —*Melody Pagan, third grade*

> I remember when I first knew myself.
> —*Courtney Blenman, fifth grade*

Family, Friends, Neighbors. Interesting or peculiar relatives, funny things about your mom or dad, sibling rivalry—all provide good material for a list poem. *Neighbors* could be considered a separate category. They can be nice but also nosy, or, sometimes, downright unpleasant. A certain Mr. . . . Cutler? Cutshaw? I can't remember. Anyway, he was an old, weird-looking guy from next door who once chased me with a rake because I rode a bike across his lawn. And just this second I remembered another neighbor, Tommy something, who was crippled and played the organ and had two huge, lazy dogs—one named Get Off the Rug and the other You Too. No kidding! Neighbors are often odd or mysterious.

> I remember when my little sister was born. My brother said that if it was a girl he was either going to run away or throw it in the garbage.
> —*Tina Santamaria, fourth grade*

> I remember giving my mother a box of raisins the day after my brother was born.
> —*Alex Covino, fourth grade*

> I remember my neighbor. He is a fool. He is my landlord.
> —*Monica Moralez, sixth grade*

> I remember when my grandmother had an operation on her feet. Day and night we were praying for her feet.
> —*Serena Camper, third grade*

> I remember when I went to my best friend Abby's birthday and gave her a safe and had Swedish meatballs.
> —*Anonymous, fourth grade*

School. Do you remember your first day in kindergarten? Did you cry? Are you still crying? What about memorable teachers (good and bad)? Formidable principals? Schoolmates—best friends, class clowns, smart kids, nerds? Who can forget school lunches? Horrendous homework? Terrifying tests? The fact that kids spend most of their waking hours in school should provide plenty of grist for the memory mill.

> I remember the first time I tried to write in script. It looked like buried mountains.
> —*Joseph Fernandez, fifth grade*

> I remember the dirtiest potatoes of my life were in the cafeteria lunch.
> —*Brad Barnes, sixth grade*

> I remember when I tried to make the letter "K."
> —*Anonymous, third grade*

I remember a boy in my class trying to take out his eyeball.
—*Sylvia Klapheck, third grade*

I remember my first day at school. I was very nervous. I bought new pencils, a new notebook, a new bookbag. I love to buy new things for school. Then I went to school and realized it wasn't so bad. I met a girl but I forgot her name. She had short blond hair with blue eyes. She was a snotty little girl but she never got snotty with me. If a person asked her to pick up their pencil she would say, "Pick it up yourself!" Nobody liked her. I was the only one. The teacher was nice. Her name was Ms. Smith. She had lots of freckles and always had a smile on her face. My friend never liked the teacher. My friend never liked anybody. Well, Ms. Smith always wore a red shirt and a navy blue skirt and glasses. My friend always got snotty with Ms. Smith. But one day my friend learned her lesson because Ms. Smith put red hot sauce in her mouth. (My friend's mother gave Ms. Smith permission.)
—*Anonymous, fifth grade*

Travel. Where have you been? What did you see and do there? Did you have any adventures? What was the food like? The landscape? The weather? What about the people—their language, dress, habits? Did you see any unusual animals? Some inner-city kids don't get too far out of their own neighborhoods, but even a trip to a local monument can yield an anecdote or two. Many students were born in foreign countries and have seen a good bit of the world. I remember (age 15) eating a banana with a knife and fork in Vienna.

I remember watching Niagara Falls being lit up with all different colored lights—probably the most beautiful thing I've ever seen. But it was too loud, much too loud. I got a headache that almost killed me.
—*Janet Searcy, sixth grade*

I remember when I first came to America. I was scared and nervous too. I couldn't find my bag with my dolls and I thought, Well that's the end of those things. Then we came onto a very big road and I was really surprised to see many thousands of Chinese people running around.
—*Roberta Singh, sixth grade*

I'll never forget when we went down south for Christmas vacation and we killed the hog, Bob. We needed more bacon and a lot of pork chops.
—*Carbon Pabon, sixth grade*

I remember when we were in Jamaica, the ugliest thing I ever saw was something brown and strange, but when I ate it, it was good!
—*Robert Johnson, fifth grade*

I remember when I went to Maine and climbed the rocks with Brian on the beach. We saw baby eagles flying and disappearing in the atmosphere.
—*Donald Downey, sixth grade*

Pets. A popular topic, this may overlap with *Sadness* (see below). When a pet dies or is given away it is often a child's first encounter with death or loss. Most kids have dogs, cats, birds, fish, hamsters (or gerbils), or, occasionally, rabbits. Then there always seems to be someone with a pet tarantula or an exotic reptile. Once again, details are important. "I remember my dog" isn't enough. What *breed* of dog are we talking about? What color? What is its personality like?

I remember my turtle who died during his third birthday. He was my companion. I still think about him, the ole whippersnapper.
—*Keenan Cooper, third grade*

I remember when my finches used to sing Mozart.
—*Juliet Ross, fifth grade*

When I was two years old I had ten dogs and they were all thirteen years old. The next day I woke up and all of them were dead. I said, "Thank God my bird isn't dead!" The next day I woke up and the bird was dead.
—*April Diaz, third grade*

I remember my snake. We named him Slinky but my brother called him Stinky. He was green and yellow and kind of skinny. He didn't do much. We still have him and he still doesn't do much.
—*Ryan Doerr, fourth grade*

I remember the pets in my house: mice, chickens, frogs, hamsters, cats, dogs, penguins, and parakeets. We are one big happy family.
—*Sabine Stone, third grade*

I have these woodchips from when my hamster was alive. All I have left of him are the memories, a picture, and the wood chips. The wood chips make me feel that my hamster's spirit still lives with me.
—*Rob Borak, eighth grade*

Toys and Clothes. Do you still have your old teddy bear? Ski sweater? G.I. Joe? Barbie? Daisy Duck feety pajamas? Some of this stuff gets handed down, some of it goes to heaven. A sub-genre of this is *Pet Blanket*, like the one Linus has in *Peanuts*. Nobody could get it away from you. You dragged it around the house until it was filthy, crusted with dried milk and goo. What color and design did it have? And you had an embarrassing name for it, too, didn't you? Blanky? Puffy?

> I had the best tap shoes. They were red. I used to put them on and tap my head off in the bathroom. Now my feet are too big for them.
> —*Andrea Grimaldi, eighth grade*

> I almost died when my mom threw away my cloth clown doll by mistake. But I had revenge! I took her earrings, a scarf, and ten dollars!
> —*Kim Smith, sixth grade*

> I remember my pet pillow. I named it Mimi. I used to drool on it every night.
> —*Michelle Vasquez, sixth grade*

> Clothes are the most important thing on my body. When I step outside I want the girls to notice me.
> —*Anonymous, fifth grade*

> I miss my pink shorts.
> —*Anonymous, fourth grade*

Accidents. Accidents can be anything from spilling soda on the new rug to getting hit by a train or blowing up the chem lab. Were you hurt? Punished? Did you go to the hospital? Did you need stitches or an operation? Any scars? In his book on children's poetry, *Moving Windows*, poet Jack Collom mentions that kids' "I Remember" poems are often "litanies of disaster." Fascination with accidents—the more grotesque or bizarre, the better—seems to be popular. This category probably comes up most often among grade school children.

> I remember when my head was coming off.
> —*Anonymous*

I remember when I jumped down ten stairs and fell right into my friend's science experiment.
  —*Eric Evans, fifth grade*

I remember the time my little sister hit me on the head. There was bleeding. What accidents I've had! And I even lost this fight to my little sister! Ridiculous!!
  —*Kam Sim Wong, eighth grade*

I remember thinking that the toaster was a bank and putting coins in the slots. My mom was almost electrocuted.
  —*Peter Brown, seventh grade*

Happy Times. These often have to do with wonderful birthday or Christmas gifts, pleasant memories of holidays or trips, visits from favorite relatives or friends, falling in (puppy) love, winning prizes or awards (see the *Proud Moments* section below), or accomplishing any difficult feat. Finding—and getting to keep—a lot of money makes kids deliriously, nervously happy. To see and hold a newborn brother or sister for the first time can be a happy experience.

I remember a happy day
When my neighbors moved far away.
  —*Anonymous*

I felt happy when I started to collect comic books. They set my imagination and mind to go wild. By the time I get a couple of million I'll be an animal, happy as happy can be. I'm a happy kid.
  —*Gene Lee Rodriguez, fourth grade*

I remember catching fish. Not a big one. But it was the only one I ever got. My father was laughing. We were all laughing.
  —*Theresa Duffy, fifth grade*

I remember one day I was walking down the street going to the store. It was the hottest day of the year. I felt like I was going to faint. I walked past a window and someone threw a bucket of ice water on me. That was one of the happiest times of my life.
  —*Crystal Shavis, seventh grade*

Sad Times. Some kids might not want to remember these, let alone write about them. For others, it can be cathartic. Be careful:

a death in the family or divorce or separation of parents can be touchy subjects to write about. Less so, but still sad or bittersweet, are the death or loss of a pet, a good friend's moving away, the loss of or damage to a favorite toy, or the deterioration of the old neighborhood. Sadness can be touching, even beautiful in an oblique way.

> I remember when I moved away from Kings Highway and I lost my best friend, Pumpkin. We always used to do the tango. It was the saddest day of my life.
> —*Kenyetta Blakely, fifth grade*

> I remember when I wasn't picked for the softball team.
> —*Eshon Furby, fifth grade*

> I remember a lot of sadness when my fish died, my cat died, my bird died, and my snake.
> —*Anonymous*

> I remember when my parents gave my dog away to Chinese people who owned many school buses.
> —*Charles Totten, fourth grade*

<u>Proud Moments</u>: taking your first step; tying your shoes all by yourself; getting a good report card; giving a speech or recital; learning to swim, to dance, to ride a bike or a horse; building an elaborate sand castle; winning a contest or a race; receiving prizes, trophies, medals. Children love to remember their accomplishments, their moments of glory. One can also be proud of what someone in one's family has achieved, or of taking part in a successful group effort.

> I remember the first time my parents trusted me and gave me the key which they never gave me before.
> —*Mai Gee Fung, eighth grade*

> I remember when I won a medal for building a palace.
> —*Wanda Leon, third grade*

> I remember when I first washed dishes, first wrote in script, ironed my own clothes. I had confidence in myself.
> —*Deprena Brady, fifth grade*

Funny Moments. These should be firsthand accounts, not something seen on television or in the movies. Pets often do amusing things. Certain people or situations can be hilarious. Practical jokes and even some accidents can seem funny to kids, even when they are the victims—more "litanies of disaster."

> The funniest thing that I ever saw was when my friends Kareem and Gene tried to measure water with a ruler.
> —*Robert Mackie, fourth grade*

> I remember the funniest thing that happened to my sister was when I sprayed starch in her mouth.
> —*Maurice Clayton, second grade*

> Once my sister Nixie was hitting me hard so I beat her up. She wasn't hurt a bit. Since she started it, my mother hit her, too. She cried like a baby and ran down the hall, slipped on some paper, fell on the floor, hit her hind, ran to her room, fell on her stomach, ran back, jumped on her bed and hit her head on the wall.
> —*Gene Lee Rodriguez, fourth grade*

> I have a funny kind of laugh, like squeaking mice, and people laugh when I laugh, so I laugh more.
> —*Valerie Nash, fifth grade*

Being Frightened. Again, these should be primary experiences. I, for one, never want to hear the name Freddy Krueger again. Or Jason. Or Michael Meyers. But Frankenstein isn't real either. *Accidents* or *Sad Times* might overlap this category. Funerals can be frightening for a young person. Being robbed or almost killed is, unfortunately, not an uncommon experience for some city children. Being left alone, especially in a dark room, is perhaps our first truly frightening moment. Hearing strange noises. Going on a first date. Being chased by a weird, rake-wielding neighbor. (See also *Being Lost* and *Dreams* below.)

> I remember standing by a fence looking at the window of a house and seeing a big fat yellow face pop up. My friend saw it too. We looked at each other and ran.
> —*Matthew Marshall, seventh grade*

I remember when I went into my bedroom and saw a strange man sleeping in my bed. I got such a pain in my heart. So I went to get my big sister and when we went close to the bed I realized it was only a pile of clothes.
—*Lena Sirovich, fifth grade*

I remember when I saw a man kill a woman.
—*Anonymous, fourth grade*

I remember being frightened by a dark shadow. It was me.
—*Tony Williams, fourth grade*

Being Embarrassed. Children can turn crimson in certain awkward situations that most adults would shrug off. When sharing these anecdotes about embarrassing moments, the teller often giggles along with the group. It's as though it happened to someone else. The importance is not in the particulars of the story but the fact that it's told at all. The act of telling is a release, a part of a communal activity, whereas the original experience of embarrassment was painful because it was isolating—one felt singled out.

I remember when a girl beat me in hand-wrestling.
—*Edgar Lopez, fourth grade*

I remember sitting in Dr. Navarre's office and a louse jumped out of my head and onto the table.
—*Anonymous, fourth grade*

I remember when my best friend forgot my name.
—*Kezzy Lewis, fourth grade*

I've been embarrassed all my life.
—*Anonymous, fifth grade*

Being Lost. To a child, it's always important to know where (and who) you are. Losing one's way or feeling even temporarily abandoned can threaten the foundation of the child's world. Almost everyone, it seems, has been lost in a stadium or a big department store. Many of us have been lost—even momentarily—in a familiar neighborhood. When you're lost, you see life from a different angle—ordinary people and things you would normally overlook now seem strangely significant.

I remember being lost at Yankee Stadium. I didn't panic. I just walked around and looked for my mom and friends. Then I sat down a while and watched the game. I remember getting hungry and I didn't have my money. I thought to myself, "It's time to be found."
—*Annalise Fremont, seventh grade*

I remember when we lost my brother at Waldbaum's. So when I was looking for him, I got lost. My dad got lost too. So we were all lost.
—*Troy Brady, fifth grade*

Losing Things: another threat to the order of one's personal universe. Depending on the value of what's lost, the experience can be worrisome or irritating, even frightening, ultimately saddening. Was it ever found? Were you able to replace it? Do you miss it still? Perhaps worst of all is to lose something precious that you borrowed from a friend or—still worse—from someone you don't know well.

I remember the time I thought I lost my silver bangle and looked everywhere, then the next day I found out Denise took it but when I asked her she said she couldn't find it. Then we all started looking for it but we couldn't find it. Then I just gave up and told Denise that I'd never speak to her again and hate her all my life. Then about a week later my mother was vacuuming and found it under the couch.
—*Scarlett Hernandez, eighth grade*

I've lost stuff all my life because I have to share a small room with my stupid brother and sister. I've lost stuff for my hair. I've lost socks, shirts, panties, and nightgowns. I even lost my church notebook and I'm having a test this week on everything I learned. I know I'm in trouble.
—*Vanessa Nieves, sixth grade*

Dreams. This potentially rich topic can stand on its own as a basis for a list poem, apart from the "I Remember" assignment. Kids tend to limit their memories of their dreams to nightmares only. This can be exciting but, just as often, cliché-ridden, peopled with stock characters (again, Freddy, Jason, et al). We mustn't neglect funny dreams, happy dreams, sad dreams, and weird (though not necessarily frightening) dreams. Daydreams count, too. A related subject is *Imaginary Friends.* It makes no difference if the dream is embellished, exaggerated, or even completely invented in the writing. The results can be just as valid, both psychologically and artistically, as an accurate recollection of a dream.

> I remember a dream about being in a telephone booth and it started shaking. Suddenly it grew wings. It flew up and dropped me into a giant cherry, raspberry, and blueberry pie. I swam around in the juice, then I was hungry. I ate and ate my way out of the pie. Then I slowly melted into dust.
> —*Roseanna Ramraj, sixth grade*

> I remember my imaginary friend Wilber. He was a little fuzzy thing. He would get me into trouble. I used to step on him.
> —*Miles Price, fifth grade*

> I dreamed I was washing a snake so my grandma could cook it. I ate a piece and it was wiggling in my stomach. When I woke up my thumb was in my mouth. I took it out fast.
> —*Kishea Carter, fifth grade*

•

Though it may seem elaborate, a brainstorm sheet of these categories, besides helping the children sort out their memories, introduces a basic principle of organization—breaking down a large subject into smaller components. We discuss each category, read examples, talk about personal memories. The teacher will, I hope, talk about her own experiences—anything of interest will do, though being embarrassed is probably the most popular topic. I ripped the seat of my pants on my first date.

Once the children finish their brainstorm sheets, they write their drafts. What category to begin with? No particular order is best. Memory should have a chance to flit about on its own. Certain areas will receive more attention than others. Not all categories apply to every student; you can't write about a pet if you've never owned one. Can't remember something? Skip it and go to a different topic.

Details are essential. Better write too much than too little:

> I remember my trip to Florida

is not enough.

> I remember my trip to Florida. I tried to feed my baloney sandwich to the alligators and one almost took my arm off

is a little better. "Baloney" helps. "There was a beautiful orange sunset with flamingoes and my sister had the mumps" would add color and variety.

I usually take home the students' drafts, select my favorite lines (everybody gets at least one), and collage them into one big *I Remember*, which I then read to the class.

> I remember when I was little and I had a pink wall. There was paint lying around and I drew a picture of a smiley face in green.
> I remember when I was on my uncle's farm all alone and every single animal got loose.
> I remember when my brothers left home for college.
> I remember when my friend told a boy I liked him and I was standing right there.
> I remember my dog Patches who always drilled holes in the lawn looking for bones.
> I remember my father in a dream yelling for no reason.
> I remember a dream of being eaten by a puppet.
> I remember when I first saw water in my life.
> I remember when we went to the hospital because I couldn't drink.
> I remember when I forgot my lines in a kindergarten play.
> I remember the first time I went out on our boat and I only put one engine in gear and we spun around in circles.
> I remember when I pretended that my pillow was a flying saucer and I fell down the stairs.
> I remember the night of my play and Paul lost his mustache.
> I remember the living dead.
> I remember when I had a dream about two men that put a machine in a woman's ear, and then when they took it out they put a song on and some worms came out of the woman's face. Then the two men saw a man and grabbed him and took him to a studio and made him look at a TV, then the song started to sing and a lot of worms came out of his face and a lot of other people died because the song came on the TV and it took their eyes off and shook their legs off.
> I remember when I was over at my grandma's house and I was riding my bicycle with my eyes closed and when I opened them I was lost.

I remember a day at my great aunt's when her friend came over. I was staring at her hair. I went to touch it and it fell off.

I remember I started sweating and then I squeaked.

I remember riding a bike and I wasn't able to turn. My whole insides turned over.

I remember a dream where my mother slammed the car door on my foot and it came off. When I woke up my foot was hanging off the side of the bed.

I remember a dream that a stick of butter was trying to kill me. (I was two inches tall.)

I remember when I got my first national touring road show—*Annie.*

I remember when I got lost in Italy.

I remember when I ran away from home and got lost and wouldn't go back until my parents came looking for me. I packed an enormous suitcase with all my stuff and could hardly carry it.

I remember when I went upstate to a dance there was a man that everyone called the "chicken man" because he had spikey hair, a funny looking nose, no sweat glands, weird looking hands, and he was really short.

I remember I lost my teddy bear Scooter with the string on his head.

I remember a dream about my whole life. I saw what I looked like when I was older—my job, my house, etc.

I remember when I got my first coin and now my collection is worth $18,000.

I remember when I was in the first grade and was taking out a book and I made a puddle at my socks.

I remember when I cut my leg open with the point of a compass (mathematical) and then had to walk 15 blocks to my house in agony.

I remember my bird that was squeezed in my sister's hands.

I remember when my father threw away my blanket.

I remember when I slept till two in the afternoon.

I remember when a friend of the family died. I was alone in the house and just finished taking a shower. The lights were off. As I walked in the room the shade flew up.

I remember climbing a pyramid in Mexico and not being brave enough to go back down.

I remember slipping and having my feet dangle over the side of the Grand Canyon.

I remember last New Year's Eve when me and my friend drank about two packs each of Coke.

I remember all the Christmases of my life.

I remember I was milking our cow Dopey and got sprayed with manure.

I remember playing ping pong with a retarded boy and losing.

I remember when the President read my letter to him in front of Congress after he was shot.

I remember my birds. First one bird flew out of the window and hit the top of a lady's umbrella. My other bird died of old age. I cried for days because I'm the only child and I used to talk to the birds.

I remember the boring hospital. I really liked bothering people in their rooms. I would take off their IV's and run.

I remember my dream about being lost in Central Park. I tripped and landed in another dimension. It was Central Park in the 1800s. I saw Sir Isaac Newton under the apple tree. When the apple was about to fall I caught it and we started floating up in the air.

Feathers was my pet bird. She was a chick. My little brat nephew squeezed her stomach and she died. We just threw her in the garbage.

I remember getting punished for an hour. When I came out of my room I was punished for two hours. After that I was punished for seven hours. Then I sneaked out my window. When I came back I was really punished.

I remember learning to stand up. I would always practice under a table and every time I stood up I bumped my head and cried.

I remember my Silly Putty walking away.

I remember watching a movie through a hurricane.

I remember when I mangled a boy.

I remember when I was four months old in my crib eating Ritz crackers with no teeth!

I remember when I was reaching up for my pinwheel on a windowsill and I slipped and the top of a Sesame Street playhouse went through my armpit.

I remember my boring trip to Taiwan with all the relatives I was supposed to remember but didn't.

I remember when I quit the viola. What a happy day!

I remember wearing feet pajamas and having a dream that my mom got her head stuck in the car seat and the windshield wipers started to chase me around and when I woke my pajamas were all twisted up and my legs were moving like windshield wipers.

I remember catching leaves as they flew in the fall.

I remember a dark midnight, April 21, 1972. I was born.

The teacher who makes a collage of kids' memories becomes, in effect, a writing partner or collaborator. Such a procedure guarantees a broad variety of details, as in a Whitman catalog, and the lines can be arranged for maximum rhythmic or dramatic effect. Students are usually fascinated by this type of group autobiography. But of course individual *I Remember* list poems can also stand quite well on their own.

Chapter 4

Oxen Should Have Very Small Foreheads
(The Lists in Sei Shonagon's Pillow Book)

Sei Shonagon was a lady-in-waiting to Empress Sadako, 1,000 years ago during the Heian period in Japan. She is the author of *The Pillow Book*, a large collection of notebooks containing diary entries, nature descriptions, portraits of court figures, gossip, anecdotes, and incidental impressions. They were jotted down in haphazard fashion throughout Shonagon's ten years' service at the Imperial Court, and kept near her bedside in the privacy of her room. She described the writing as "odd facts, stories from the past, and all sorts of other things, often including the most trivial material. . . . I concentrated on things and people that I found charming and splendid; my notes are also full of poems and observations on trees and plants, birds and insects." The poems were disappointingly conventional, but the great scholar Arthur Waley called her "the best poet of her time, a fact that is apparent only in her prose."

Obviously intelligent, lively, complex, quick-witted, sensitive to beauty and the most minute phenomena, Shonagon was also a terrific snob. "I cannot stand a woman who wears sleeves of unequal width," she once wrote. She adored the Imperial Family and was often downright callous in her scorn for the lower classes. On occasion, she could be hostile to men. That she set herself apart from the crowd is clearly stated at the end of her book: "I am the sort of person who approves of what others abhor and detests the things they like."

Shonagon was a fanatical list-maker. *The Pillow Book* contains 164 lists, many with commentary or description. Her topics include: *Things That Make One's Heart Beat Faster; Clouds; Poetic Subjects* ("Hail, bamboo grass"); *Rare Things; Oxen Should Have Very Small Foreheads; Things That Arouse a Fond Memory of the Past* ("Last year's paper fan"); *Unsuitable Things* ("Ugly handwriting on red paper");

Insects ("I feel very sorry for the basket worm"); *Things That Have Lost Their Power, Things That Give a Hot Feeling; Different Ways of Speaking; Illnesses; Things That Are Near Though Distant; People Who Seem to Suffer; Things That Give a Clean Feeling*. This potpourri of themes is unified by Shonagon's concise, limpid prose style.

Elegant Things

A white coat worn over a violet waistcoat.
Duck eggs.
Shaved ice mixed with liana syrup and put in a new silver bowl.
A rosary of rock crystal.
Wisteria blossoms. Plum blossoms covered with snow.
A pretty child eating strawberries.

Things That Give a Clean Feeling

An earthen cup. A new metal bowl.
A rush mat.
The play of light on water as one pours it into a vessel.
A new wooden chest.

Things That Give an Unclean Feeling

A rat's nest.
Someone who is late in washing his hands in the morning.
White snivel, and children who sniffle as they walk.
The containers used for oil.
Little sparrows.
A person who does not bathe for a long time even though the water is hot.
All faded clothes give me an unclean feeling, especially those that have glossy colors.

Adorable Things

The face of a child drawn on a melon.
A baby sparrow that comes hopping up when one imitates the squeak of a mouse, or again, when one has tied it with a thread round its leg and its parents bring insects or worms and pop them in its mouth—delightful!

A baby of two or so is crawling rapidly along the ground. With his sharp eye he catches sight of a tiny object and, picking it up with his pretty little fingers, takes it to show a grownup person.

A child, whose hair has been cut like a nun's, is examining something; the hair falls over his eyes, but instead of brushing it away he holds his head to one side. The pretty white cords of his trouser-skirt are tied round his shoulders, and this too is most adorable.

A young Palace page, who is still quite small, walks by in ceremonial costume.

One picks up a pretty baby and holds him for a while in one's arms; while one is fondling him, he clings to one's neck and then falls asleep.

The objects used during the Display of Dolls.

One picks up a tiny lotus leaf that is floating on a pond and examines it. Not only lotus leaves, but little hollyhock flowers, and indeed all small things, are most adorable.

An extremely plump baby, who is about a year old and has a lovely white skin, comes crawling towards one, dressed in a long gauze robe of violet with the sleeves tucked up.

A little boy of about eight reads aloud from a book in his childish voice.

Pretty, white chicks who are still not fully fledged and look as if their clothes are too short for them; cheeping loudly, they follow one on their long legs, or walk close to the mother hen.

Duck eggs.

An urn containing the relics of some holy person.

Wild pinks.

In the spirit of Sei Shonagon, American poet Philip Whalen (coincidentally a Zen monk) has written, in an off-the-cuff vernacular, a number of list poems that seem like updates of *The Pillow Book*.

Ultimate Frivolous Necessities
for Nemi Frost

1. Bamboo trees
2. marble
3. crystals and other semiprecious stones & little objects made out of these materials
4. silk
5. bells

6. big palaces near the sea
    a) Knossos
    b) Cintra
    c) Kamakura
    d) Cozumel
    e) The California Palace of the Legion of Honor
    f) Bebe Rebozo's place in Florida
7. fur
8. amber
9. incense
10. gin
11. dope
12. Baccarat crystal
13. Peacock feathers

                    11:VIII:67

Another contemporary poet, Anne Waldman, had an interesting idea for a list poem:

Things That Go Away & Come Back Again

Thoughts
Airplanes
Boats
Trains
People
Dreams
Animals
Songs
Husbands
Boomerangs
Lightning
The sun, the moon, the stars
Bad weather
The seasons
Soldiers
Good luck
Health
Depression
Joy
Laundry

I once asked my students in a college poetry workshop to write, as a means of getting acquainted, a list of fifty things they liked a lot. (We also wrote lists of what we didn't like.) Fifty is a high enough number to ensure variety. Alison Burns's response covers a broad spectrum of abstract concepts and concrete images:

the land	sari lounging
black	national forests
walking	listening
driving large cars	leading people
dirt floors	early morning fresh fruit
dreaming	holding books
the ocean	reading
backpacking	Pernod
crowds	kindness
amusing men	to play
onyx	my writing
olives	experiments
private libraries	people watching
relaxing on mountaintops	airports
three weeks camping	masquerade parties
dogs following me	music
movies	intimate friends
devastating dresses	antiques
gracious women	marble
old houses	ancient graveyards
gentlemen	window seats
madcap journeys	intense discussion
grapevines	animals
jasmine	lace (black)
rich travel	revolution

This is quite a contrast with Anne Waldman's very particular theme. Alison's poem was composed on the spot; the order is random and there's a little overlapping. The items veer from the general (play, experiments, listening, music) to the precise (Pernod, jasmine, dirt floors, window seats, olives). One can appreciate the distinction between "holding books" and "reading." And "sari lounging" sounds like exotic fun.

Feather pillows, full moon, memories, cleansing cream, black (lace, velvet, ribbon, dress), mermaids, first cigarette when I wake up, Korean pottery, Big Mac, old theatre, Rocky Mountains, wild trees, vapor trails, shadow of the clouds, bridges over rivers, clear sky on a chilly night, signal at sunrise and sunset, red lipstick, Japanese old vocabulary, ruby-colored drinks, candles, pearl necklaces, tulips, piano, white linen, fragrance, crystal glasses, backstage, swings, 50¢ coffee from the deli, discords, balance (space, rhythm, color, movement), high ceilings, continuous numbers, chocolate cake with milk, outdoor swimming pools at night, white radish, poppies, hot baths, supermarkets, Evian water, letters, rivers, matches, school uniforms, white walls, blue lights, boxwood combs, big windows, shadow of myself on the wall.

—*Kumiko Ueki*

This "50 Things" poem by another workshop member has a fragile, floating (dare I say Shonagonesque?) quality. Kumiko, who was born in Portland, Oregon, and raised in Japan and India, mixes her Eastern and Western sensibilities here. "Big Mac" creates a thud, coming just after "Korean pottery." I love the oddness of some choices (continuous numbers, cleansing cream, school uniforms). "Discords" refers to music, but I'm not sure what the "signal at sunrise" can be.

This poem by Valery Larbaud could be called "Thirty-Six Things I Like a Lot":

Alma Perdida

To you, vague aspirations; enthusiasms;
Thoughts after lunch; emotional impulses;
Feelings that follow the gratification
Of natural needs; flashes of genius; agitation
Of the digestive process; appeasement
Of good digestion; inexplicable joys;
Circulatory problems; memories of love;
Scent of benzoin in the morning tub; dreams of love;
My tremendous Castilian joking, my vast
Puritan sadness, my special tastes;
Chocolate, candies, so sweet they almost burn; iced drinks;
Drowsy cigars; you, sleepy cigarettes;
Joys of speed; sweetness of being seated; excellence

Of sleeping in total darkness;
Great poetry of banal things; news items; trips;
Gypsies; sleigh rides; rain on the sea;
Delirium of feverish night, alone with a few books;
Ups and downs of temperature and temperament;
Recurring moments from another life; memories, prophecies;
O splendors of the common life and the usual this and that,
To you this lost soul.
    —*Translated by Bill Zavatsky and Ron Padgett*

"50 Things I Like" may not be the best assignment for young children. Why? Their limited experience might result in less diversified and detailed catalogs. Yet, diversity itself can be taught and used as a basis of list poems, as seen in the *I Remember* assignment. I've tried using other generalized themes for lists, such as beauty, ugliness, and sadness; they've worked fairly well, especially when I've taken dictation on the blackboard from an entire class:

Poem of Beauty

The beautiful poem
The beautiful flower that grows on earth
The beautiful name of tulips
The beautiful little girl planting the roses
The beautiful cookies in the jar
The pretty green headband of the Chinese girl
The cute little shirt—red with blue and orange stripes
Beautiful Chinese food
Beautiful Americans eating pork chops
Beautiful sky
Beautiful birds sinking in it
Leaves fall on the sidewalk
Extremely beautiful women with make-up (blush, shadow, powder)
    buying perfume, jewelry, wallpaper, shelf paper—black shelf
    paper in their minds—foods, a turtle, several things they think
    about
The beautiful men
The baseball with its beautiful beige bat
Beautiful girl, boy, rabbit, kitten, monkey, bear
The most beautiful small things are pencils, marbles, dominoes, mice,
    glue

Lovely sandwiches
Beautiful dreams of Christmas, gorgeous Christmas
Colors of the flag
Beautiful valentine
The beautiful chocolate clock
The beautiful heart that ticks
Beautiful star in the night
Special as the moon's banana face
Beautiful days go by so fast like gold bullets
Time: 5 o'clock
Place: the park
Characters: Bugs Bunny, G.I. Joe
Bugs: Beautiful sweetheart . . .
Joe: Come to me, dear . . .
Bugs: She's mine!
Joe: No, she's mine!
The beautiful fist fight between G.I. Joe and Bugs Bunny for the
    beautiful girl named
Elizabeth
Elizabeth Taylor
Her tongue is a beautiful snake
The beautiful old television that broke down and turned into spaghetti
    and clam sauce
The pen with its beautiful ink
The beautiful end
    —*Third grade class*

I usually encourage students to avoid easy, dull adjectives in their writing, but here the repetition of *beautiful* creates a hypnotic, rhythmic quality, a kind of singing, that enhances rather than cheapens the poem. (*Cute, lovely,* and *special* make token appearances to vary the effect.) Sei Shonagon continually used *okashi* (charming) and *medetashi* (splendid) as refrains to achieve similar rhythm or mood.

The subject is announced in the title and the poem itself is characterized in the first line. With that out of the way, the third graders began their catalog with flowers. Upon my request, they added more detail (roses, tulips) and continue down to the splendid simile of days passing "like gold bullets." The list stops here to consider time, neatly segues to a miniature play or TV soap opera, and wraps itself up reflexively.

Here's another "poem by committee," this one by a half-dozen fourth graders

Beautiful

I am beautiful
So are you
He isn't so beautiful
She is only kind of beautiful
That dog is really ugly
What is really beautiful?
Butterflies with their pink and orange spots are beautiful
Roses blooming in a pot in the spring
Hamburgers dripping with ketchup, pickles, and onions are beautiful
    when you're starving to death in front of McDonald's
Imani is beautiful right now
She will be beautiful tomorrow
And forever
Coney Island is beautiful with rides and games, sand and waves, treats
    and prizes
Those beautiful green waves are rapid and salty
Stars when they glow in the darkness like Winnie's eyes are extremely
    beautiful
Kittens when they roll a ball of yarn and make a big mess in your living
    room
Beautiful purple screaming firecrackers
Gleaming jumping jacks
Santa Claus when he shoots down the chimney and plops like Jello at
    the bottom
Circus clowns smiling you to the wacko house
Your beautiful heart pounding important blood through all the
    sections of your big fat body
Hair in a pom pom
Hair in a flattop
Hair in a gumby
Hair in a twist
Dances of all the states are wonderful
The Georgia Break
The Mississippi Backflip
The Alabama Lambada
The Connecticut Hula
The Virginia Bump

The Kentucky Funky Chicken
The Texas Electric Slide
The Louisiana Bus Stop
The California Heartbeat
And the extremely elegant ballet of the nations all across the concrete
    surface of the earth
Just beautiful!
Ducks as they wobble into their slimy pond
Lightning bugs lighting up as you sit on a bench and stare into the night
The beauty of milk
The beauty of lowfat ham
Gorgeous girls with lips of glass
Cute little baby blue jays
Pretty bunnies hopping in your flower garden
Nice old fat ladies with baskets of candies
Handsome men and boys in ties and pants
Perfect circles
Special insects with bubbling backs and sticky antennae
Neon hats
Quiet lakes
Helpful schools
Superman rejects
Rap and reggae
Colorful balls bouncing down the stairs
Yo-yos
G.I. Joes
Fingers and toes
Rainbows so bright your eyes go blank
Black Beauty
The Beast who is a very nice protector for the woman who loves him
    even though nobody else can stand him
Designs of shapes and colors that sparkle in silent museums
Painters with their beautiful brushes making bowls of fruit to entertain
    and please the people
Good teachers are beautiful
Money—but only if it's used right
Sleep is the most beautiful thing when your bones need to stretch out
    on cool sheets
My mother is really beautiful
In fact, just about everything can be beautiful
If you give it a chance
    —Carlton Selby, Gregory Hamberry, David Lee Waters, Imani Prysock,
    Winnie Burgess, Ruth Kendall

Despite its conventional ending, "Beautiful" is perhaps even more dynamic than "Poem of Beauty." At the end of the delightful minilist of dances, it peaks in a Whitmanesque crescendo with the "extremely elegant ballet of the nations." Then, the more varied catalog starts up again and, along the way, we encounter some strange surprises: "Neon hats," "lips of glass," "bubbling backs." I guess someone thought of "lowfat ham" as a beauty aide.

Of course, children manage on their own to write fine list poems with a mixture of images:

The Ten Ugliest Things in the World

1. lady with gun
2. spinach
3. my butt
4. Tricia or Chantell
5. glasses
6. lunch
7. Haiti
8. frog
9. wine
10. my boyfriend
   —*Naomi White, second grade*

Beautiful Things

flowers
Kimberly
ladybugs
pools
Mrs. Carlson
boats
spaceships
tulips
flags
haircuts
dresses
planets
babies
pandas
   —*Jason Velez, fourth grade*

Ten Beautiful Things

puppies
people with manners
my body
Queen Elizabeth
performances
jewelry
gardens
glory
learning
black shoes
    —*Jakanta Leggett, sixth grade*

How Beautiful the Pine Tree Is

How beautiful the pine tree is
How beautiful the pussycats
How beautiful my old black BMX bike
How beautiful my clean house
How beautiful THE FESTIVAL OF FAIRY TALES
How beautiful my little leather basketball
How beautiful my friends—tall Rollo and kind Pooh Bear
My slim Uncle Benny
How beautiful (anyway) my sister Tamika the Bully
My beautiful father who gave me Fila sneakers
My beautiful old grandmother down south
How beautiful my black-white-pink-blue-yellow suit of clothes
How beautiful my drawings of Bart Simpson
How beautiful my dear old funny fifth grade class
How beautiful my little desk in that class
How beautiful the fruit—furry peaches, big pink watermelon
How beautiful some candy—apple-flavored Now Laters
How beautiful the orange juice that builds up my protein
How beautiful the dish of apple sauce
How beautiful Bugs Bunny who dresses as a lady and when men kiss
    him he changes back into himself and the men wipe their mouths
    off
How beautiful my building—they just started cleaning it up
How beautiful are shrimps
How beautiful my cat
How beautiful ME—for my own friendship
    —*Earl Jones, fifth grade*

The Most Beautiful Things I Can Think of Are:

diamonds
rubies
bronzes
gold
emeralds
lightning bugs
ladybugs
turkey
chicken
                    &
science
      —*Alan Lewis, third grade*

More Ugly Things

frogmonster
the pupa
ham & pumpkin seed sandwich
a duck eating a worm
Hurricane Hugo
a bad black dracula pig
the liver inside your stomach
ripped-up dress
a collection of bloody toys
stabbing a baby
stabbing Martin Luther King, Jr.
      —*Candice Sealey, second grade*

Yikes! Sometimes second graders really let it all hang out. Children, as a rule, love grotesque imagery; they are masters of the yucky. Still, a topic like *ugly* often leads to mere self-indulgence and predictable silliness. So beware.

There is only a brief entry on *sadness* in the *The Pillow Book* ("To Feel That One Is Disliked by Others"). I'm surprised Shonagon didn't deal more thoroughly with such a basic human emotion. An inner-city fifth grade group, writing mainly from firsthand experience, inventoried a broad spectrum of sad things, from dismay (food stains—many kids take these quite seriously) to despair (a death in the family):

Sadness

Seeing the summer go away
Seeing the birds fly away
Seeing the butterflies die in the spring
Seeing my best friend move away
Seeing black and white people getting beat up by the Ku Klux Klan
Seeing people in the street
With nothing to eat
And nowhere to go
And nothing to do
Seeing my mother go away on a business trip to Florida
Seeing people across the street getting burnt out because someone set
    their house on fire
Seeing the old movie theater getting knocked down by construction
    men
Seeing my sisters and brothers leaving for camp in the summer
Seeing China choke on her turkey sandwich
The death of babies when their mother throws them out of a 10th-floor
    window
Or sticks them in a garbage compactor
You are taken away from your family and friends
Your mother screams bloody murder
You and your friends get money
But it isn't yours
And you lose it
You lie to your mother and she finds out
Your grandfather dies
Sadness is when a poor dog has a broken leg
Or skin disease
It is sad when your grandmother is sick in the hospital
It breaks your heart to see people die
When your mother and father fight—that is sad
It is sad to see a retarded person
Or to see a little girl or boy being abused by their parents
When you go on punishment, can't go anywhere
The people who died in Vietnam
Little birds that get run over on the Atlantic Expressway
When you die just because of the color of your skin

Young teenagers getting raped for no reason
People that get beat up very badly
Just because someone in their class
Didn't like the way he or she acted
People who don't get promoted
Children and adults who can't read
Broken toys never used again
Blindness—never to see the sun and stars
Ink spots or food stains on clean white shirts
Bad education in some of the schools
These sad times
Dirt and pollution falling out of the sky
Onto everyone and everything
Fake hair for baldheaded ladies
The drugs on the street
The drugs in the projects
The drugs in the marijuana trees
Death to the people
Death in Bensonhurst
Death to unfortunate crack babies
Stupid pregnant teenage users
Libraries closing down
People can't learn about history and life
Bulldozers knocking down your property
Little kids playing with guns under their mother's bed
Crazy crackheads beating on their wives, girlfriends, children, pets
Cruelty of children to each other
Decepticons coming at you in evil headbands
Graffiti spoiling all the sights
What a sad world
What a sad time

    —Desiree Bell, China Leigh, Barbara Sloan, Tiffany Hunter, Melinda Witters

A second grader wrote the following:

Sadness

Sadness for my grandmother who died a couple of days ago
Sadness like Michael Jackson's song "Man in the Mirror"
Sadness of Valentino, who pulled down everybody's coats and broke
    the door (He will be beaten with belts)

Sadness of poor homeless lady bums with nothing to eat or drink
Sadness of fat boys who behave like fools
Sadness of chicken disrupters
Sadness of starving babies in Africa skinny as invisible ribs
Sadness of being alone in the house for a while
Sadness of having no friends
Sadness of being too small to get a job
Sadness for my teacher who fell downstairs
Sadness for little Wah San who can speak no English and is sometimes
 afraid
Sadness of dark dreams
Sadness of broken chairs
Sadness of screaming in the lunchroom (I can't even hear myself
 crunching my own potato chips!)
Sadness of church bells
Sadness of funerals
Sadness of getting married—tears got all over my dress
Sadness of almost everything
Except when you are near
And we play our game of writer
 —*Laguirre Wearing*

Shonagon *does* make a big fuss about "Things without Merit" ("rice starch mixed with water"), "Squalid Things" ("the inside of a cat's ear"), "Presumptuous Things" ("coughing," "spoiled children"), unpleasant, distressing, annoying things—things that drove her crazy.

Things That Drive Me Crazy

my brother, my girlfriend, fashion shows, long essays, constipation, headaches, rats, jeri curls, hospitals, strict teachers, stuck-up girls, cod liver oil, when I can't find anything, grandma, police sirens, certain things my nephew does, heavy metal music, spiked hair, dogs that bark too much, anchovies, sushi, sardines, George Bush, hair on my legs, Wednesday, bright colors, math, phone ringing when I'm home alone in the bath, when a baby lies and gets away with it, movies that never let me see the bad guy, cross-eyed people, all the killing, all the drugs, all the raping, cute boys, cost of things, when white people talk about the things blacks can't do, people who argue under my bedroom window at four in the morning, when babies step on me with those hard shoes, cleaning my room, my cat, taking out the trash, homework,

when my favorite TV show doesn't come on, when my mother buys something ugly, when the strap pops off my bookbag, people dissing you for nothing, when the sequels to movies get more boring each time, people popping their gum, when you're standing right next to someone and they still talk too loud, people who ask the same thing over and over, not having money, people getting something I want, people who tap on things, when my friends come over and never know when to leave.
—*Seventh grade class*

Things That Drive Me Crazy

people who talk too much
people who laugh too much
people who laugh too loud
parents who worry too much
my friends
boyfriends
fear
acting in the wrong
acting like someone you're not
banks
supermarkets
people who can't cook
missing school
having a mean teacher
my brother throwing pennies at me in the night
too many lights on in the house
drugs
deep water
rubber ducks
mixed vegetables
—*Yolanda Spivey, sixth grade*

The philosopher-poet Max Picard wrote *The World of Silence*, a book in which practically every sentence includes the word *silence*. The subject is the healing quality of silence in a world of noise and chatter. The writing style is haunting.

Sometimes, when the wall of a house stands in the light of noon, it is as though the light were taking possession of the wall on behalf of silence. One can feel the approach of the silence of the noonday heat. The light lies firmly on the wall as a sign that the wall belongs to the silence.

The gate in the wall is shut; the windows are covered with curtains; people inside the house are very quiet, as though they were lowering their heads at the approach of the silence.

The inside wall seems to expand through the silence pressing upon it.

Then suddenly a song lights up on the wall from inside. The notes are like bright balls thrown at the wall. And now it is as though the silence rises from the wall and climbs upward towards the sky, and the windows in the wall are like the steps of a ladder leading the silence and also the song into the sky above.

The following third grade collaboration has something of Picard's (and Shonagon's) lucid, contemplative feeling:

Quiet

Restaurants are quiet when people are dating
A motel is very quiet
In the dark there is always quiet
A snake is silent
An ant is quiet
It's quiet in the park
A lamp is quiet
A window is quiet
It's quiet when you go to your house by yourself
It is quiet when your mother is sleeping
Rabbits are quiet
It's quiet in church
Winter is quiet
The library is very quiet
The quiet deer
Slowly moments are quiet
A hotel is quiet
The sun is quiet
A harp is quiet
A lizard is quiet
A turtle is quiet
Plants are quiet
My friend Mary is peaceful and quiet
The moon is quiet
  —*Third grade group*

Chapter 5

Parts of the Body

We know about children's fascination with the weird, the marvelous, the fantastic, and the fabulous. Monsters, giants, chimeras, and mythological beasts are staples of children's literature. Why not let kids build their own Frankensteins? It's easy: just start at the top with the hair and go straight down to the toes (avoiding, if necessary, the controversial bits along the way). Or you can mix it all up. "Arnold" is a chimera, compounded strictly from parts of animals:

Arnold

The legs of a turkey
The eyes of a snake
The stomach of a turtle
The ears of a goose
The toes of a lion
The heart of a goat
The smile of a cow
The feet of a penguin
The lips of a duck
The elbows of an emu
The shoulders of a fly
The neck of an owl
The eyebrows of a rhinoceros
The chest of a pelican
The knees of a wolf
The back of a cat
The ears of a giraffe
The ankles of a hippo
The teeth of a pig
The hair of a skunk
The cheeks of a chicken
The chin of a reindeer
The personality of a jackal
   —Fourth grade class

I guess it's okay for Arnold to have two sets of ears. He's nice, but how about *these* extravagant concoctions?

Grandpa Dynamite

Hair like sticks of dynamite
Forehead like a pistachio basketball
Eyebrows like velvet frankfurters
Eyes like corduroy bowling balls
Nose like a bloodshot needle
Ears like silk hamburgers
Mustache like a corncob worm
Mouth like a rubber racetrack
Teeth like silver flagpoles
Tongue like a green glass zipper
Anchovy chin
Neck like a drunken flowerpot
Shoulders like the Swiss Alps
A chest like the frozen sea
Arms like singing umbrellas
    (singing "Singin' in the Rain")
Legs like bagels of moonlight
Feet like simet lopserts (cement lobsters)
    —*Fourth grade class*

Monsieur America (The Last Monster)

He's got
Hair like chocolate Christmas lights
A forehead like a radio playing music as soft as Breakstone Butter
Eyes like 17 lead meatballs
Ears like Transylvanian sneakers
A nose like a lawnmower of chicken skin
A mustache like strips of black pancreas
Teeth like 167,000 diamond doorbells
A tongue like the equator (a steaming hot line around the globe)
A chin like a leather mosquito
A chest like old Texas
Arms like seesaws at the seashore
A stomach like a tarpit in inner space

Frogs legs in Bernaise
Feet like glass sinks of gunpowder
A personality like an epileptic torpedo
   —*Third grade class*

Doctor Harold Sinister

Hair like licorice dictionaries
Forehead like a cement grapefruit
Eyes like rubber mothballs
Nose like a steel box of kleenex
Ears like turquoise frying pans of perfumed air
Mustache like a can of Schlitz
Lips like string beans wrapped in newspaper
Teeth like a cob of candy corn
Tongue like a seven dollar bill
Neck like a Hungarian staircase
Arms like the Washington Monument and Jefferson Memorial
Hands like polka-dot wedding bells
Chest like an umbrella with the mumps
Stomach like somebody else's universe
Frogs' legs in crab sauce followed by crabs in soy sauce
Feet like rooks on a Monopoly board
Personality of an inchworm
   —*Fourth grade class*

This assignment works best as a group construction project, kids teaming up to create catalogs of "wondrous strange" similes. However, we can't expect every line to be a knockout. Kids tend to get bogged down in one type of simile or metaphor. You'll notice a preponderance of food/flavor imagery.

As for precedents for the "monster" poem, nothing can beat the many prose catalogs to be found in Rabelais's *Gargantua and Pantagruel*. For example, King Lent's Adam's apple is

> like a barrel, his beard is like a lantern, his chin like a mushroom, his
> ears like mittens, his eyebrows like dripping pans, his cheeks . . . a pair
> of wooden shoes . . . teeth . . . like so many stout staves . . . his toes
> suggest the keyboard of a spinet, his nails gimlets, his heels clubs, his
> soles crucibles, his legs bird snares, his knees stools . . . tongue . . . like

a harp, his mouth like a horsecloth, his face is embroidered like a mule's packsaddle, his head is fashioned like a still, his skull like a gamepouch [. . .]

Rooting around in my archive of body-part similes by kids, I found an assortment equal to that of Rabelais. I will now attempt to build my own monster out of these stray metaphors:

Premier El Abdul Irving Unusual IV

Hair like millions of Chinese janitors
A forehead like a sharkskin bowling ball
Eyes like a vampire's beachballs
A nose like tunnels of Brillo
Ears like frozen whirlpools
Teeth like miniature rusty lawnmowers
A tongue like a butterfly in a tarpit
One fat lip
Arms like golden bed warmers
A chest like an ironing board with chicken pox
Legs like chickenskin popsicles
A stomach like an ocean of ghosts
Feet like suction cups of tea
A mustache like a wool ladyfinger
A neck like a worm-infested coathanger

Irving is ugly enough. You might want to encourage your students to create beautiful monsters, too.

One type of list poem is the *blazon* (or *blason*), which originated in sixteenth-century France. Though some are short and satiric, most blazons are longer catalogs of similes that celebrate and praise some part or parts of the female body, as in the following Elizabethan excerpt from Lord Herbert of Cherbery:

A Description

I sing her worth and praises high,
    Of whom a poet cannot lie,
The little world the great shall blaze;[1]
Sea, earth, her body; heaven, her face;
Her hair, sunbeams; whose every part

71

Lightens, enflames, each lover's heart:
That thus you prove the axiom[2] true,
Whilst the sun help'd nature in you.

    Her front,[3] the white and azure sky,
In light and glory raised high,
Being o'ercast by a cloudy frown,
All hearts and eyes dejecteth down.

    Her each brow a celestial bow,
Which through this sky her light doth show,
Which doubled, if it strange appear,
The sun's likewise is doubled there.

    Her either cheek a blushing morn,
Which, on the wings of beauty born,
Doth never set, but only fair
Shineth, exalted in her hair.

    Within her mouth, heaven's heav'n, reside
Her words, the soul's there glorifi'd.

    Her nose th'equator of this globe,
Where nakedness, beauty's best robe,
Presents a form all hearts to win.

    Last nature made that dainty chin [. . .]

(Notes:
[1]*blaze:* blazon.
[2]*the axiom:* "Man's parents are man and the sun."
[3]*front:* forehead.)

A well-known modern (1931) example is by the French surrealist poet André Breton, which begins:

Free Union
(excerpt)

My woman with her forest-fire hair
With her heat-lightning thoughts
With her hourglass waist
My woman with her otter waist in the tiger's mouth
My woman with her rosette mouth a bouquet of stars of the greatest
    magnitude
With her teeth of white mouse footprints on the white earth
With her tongue of polished amber and glass

My woman with her stabbed eucharist tongue
With her tongue of a doll that opens and closes its eyes
With her tongue of incredible stone
My woman with her eyelashes in a child's handwriting
With her eyebrows the edge of a swallow's nest
My woman with her temples of a greenhouse with a slate roof
And steam on the windowpanes
My woman with her shoulders of champagne
And a dolphin-headed fountain under ice
My woman with her matchstick wrists
My woman with her lucky fingers her ace of hearts fingers
With her fingers of new-mown hay [. . .]
    —*Translated by Bill Zavatsky and Zack Rogow*

Children's blazons aren't always complimentary.

To My Love

Your eyes are like marbles rolling in your head.
Your smile is like sweet potato pie.
Your nose is like a tunnel full of bears.
Your shoulders are as soft as pillowcases.
Your neck is as pink as bubble gum.
Your legs are as hairy as a fox fur.
Your arms look as if you were a wrestler.
Your hair blows in the wind like a balloon drifting.
Your legs are as white as cream.
Your feet are as big as loaves of bread.
Your neck is like the scent of Downy.
Your neck is as long as my passion for you.
Your legs are as flexible as rubber.
Your teeth are like icicles hanging from the rooftop.
Your smile is like the opening of a box.
Your arms are like a spinning wheel.
Your hair is as greasy as corn oil.
Your eyes look like peas in a pod.
Your lips flutter like two giant window shades.
Your nose is as long as a tree branch.
Your smile is as weak as a dried-up leaf.
Your hands are like fly swatters.
Your toes look like jangling keys.
    —*Roseanna Ramraj, Norma Rodriguez, Melissa Medina, Isabel Co-
    lon, Monica Moralez, Osvaldo Morales, and Earl McClellan, sixth grade*

This mixture of pretty, ugly, strange, sweet, practical ("flexible legs"), and commercial ("Downy") also contains a rather mature metaphor ("Your neck is as long as my passion for you"). A kinder, gentler poem by a second grade trio:

A Harp of Happiness

Your brains are intelligent basketballs with antennae
Your hair is sexy blue dandelions
Your eyes are sparkling glass marbles
Your lips are two orange plastic snakes
Your chin is a little sofa
Your cheeks are warm cotton bread
Your breath is strawberry smoke
Your teeth are Japanese hummingbird eggs
Your ears are goatskin bongo drums
Your nose is a squeezable soda machine
Your arms are automatic bananas
Your heart is a soft kitten of wishes
Your face is Jupiter's bright moon
Your smile is a harp of happiness
Your neck is a gorgeous roll of tissue
Your head is the globe of Venus
Your shoulders are tender ocean waves
Your arms are loving green woolen cobras
Your fingers are chocolate mint worms
Your legs are silver space trains
Your knees are melons with prizes inside
Your feet are dancing cake mixers
Your toes are Egyptian McNuggets
     —Natalie Neckles, Rosanka Saintcy, and Steven Cavallos

One needn't stick strictly to parts of the body to write catalog verse in praise of a loved one. Other endearing attributes can be added. In Gershwin's "They Can't Take That Away from Me," Fred Astaire, singing to Ginger Rogers, itemizes her wonderful manner of doing things: "The way you wear your hat/the way you sip your tea . . . The way your smile just beams/the way you sing off-key/the way you haunt my dreams . . ." Cole Porter's brilliant sequence of metaphors in his song "You're the Top" compares the beloved to "the Colosseum . . . the Louvre Museum . . . a Waldorf salad . . . a

Berlin ballad" and so on. More obliquely, in Link, Strachey, and Marvell's song "These Foolish Things," the singer is reminded of his departed lover by "a cigarette that bears a lipstick's traces/an airline ticket to romantic places," and other details that resonate. These are all examples of great list-making in popular music.

Though today most kids are less squeamish than ever before about showing affection for someone of the opposite sex, some just can't resist a little subtle (and not so subtle) needling, combining sincerity and irony in their poems.

Reasons to Love You

You have no friends
You're different than everyone else
You're brilliant
You can't swim
You're deliciously cute and so lusciously annoying
My heart's on fire
It's your birthday
You got a 60 on your math test
Your ears wiggle
I'm boy crazy
You make beds
You love to take the garbage out
Your write your words backwards
You wear tight black pants
You eat little flowers
You don't belong on the earth
I'm crazy
My aunt is your godmother
Your last name is interesting
Your head is not very big
You pay attention to me
You cook pancakes
You can't write poems
  —*Fourth grade group*

Why I Love You

You have clean hands
It's raining
My dog died

75

The customer is always right
Your car is so big I can fit my clothes into it
You know how to throw a football
      —*Lena Williamson, fifth grade*

Reasons to Love You

Our frogs kissed
You understand the way I feel
I can't cook
Your skin feels like glass
You look like a Siberian lynx
I have nothing better to do
Your check didn't bounce
Our parents set us up
Our love is perpetual
I am weird
I just love you
You're adorable
You're sitting on my chewing gum
      —*Jason Singleton and James Tillman, fifth grade*

Valentine's Day is probably the optimum occasion for writing
and receiving love poems. Some eighth grade students prepared for
a collaborative valentine by reading and discussing Elizabeth Barrett
Browning's famous sonnet, beginning "How do I love thee? Let me
count the ways." Their poem is a complex of refrains and metaphors,
a list that starts and ends with explosive hyperbole:

A Valentine

For I love you so much that I would give anything to see your beautiful
      white face in the giant red-orange sunset
And for your love I would take your picture, frame it, and put it on a
      silver plate
And I love you like I love my dreams
And for your love I would cast a shadow upon all those who contain
      hate
Yes, for your great love I would jump in front of a Pinto but you would
      bless me so I don't get to be in the hospital
I can't go one minute without seeing your face

And I love you like a mother loves her crippled child
And I need your love like glass needs a hammer
Like a bird needs a suit
Like a baby needs curlers
Like bears need an alarm clock
Like bees need a spelling book
Like butterflies need gas
Yes, for you I would kiss the ground you walk on, cherish your
    thoughts, cuddle your mind!
I love you so much that my heart is withering away with the flowers
    I gave you last evening
And for your love I would make a necklace out of the biggest stars up
    in the sky
And I love you like I would love a soft pillow
For your love I would waltz barefoot on a porcupine
For your love I would understand a purple tarantula
For your love I would slip on a banana peel and stop in mid-air
For your love I would sing with the Royal Canadian Mounties
And I love you like I love my own parents
And for your love I would swim across the Atlantic Ocean in a lead
    bathing suit
And I love you like the poor old man who everyone has forgotten loves
    the tomb!
And I love you like
You love to watch
The stones following
The stream so blindly
And I love you like Josephine (Logenheimer) loves Napoleon
    (Steinbaum)
And I love you like mosquitoes love sweet red blood
And for your love I would fight all the bulls with a red kleenex
And for your love I would eat a rightside-up cake standing upside-
    down
For my love is greater than dynamite or even a lollipop, it's just so
    beautiful that I can't stop watching your excellent hair going by!

Returning once more to our anatomy lesson, Kenneth Koch's
wonderful "Faces," inspired by Walt Whitman's poem of the same
name, is neither monster nor love poem, but a long parade of faces
belonging to almost anyone or anything—famous people, generic
types, fictional characters, animals, plants, inanimate objects, whole
cities, even abstract ideas. Many are merely named, some are

described in detail, some are involved in extended metaphors. Here are some excerpts:

> The face of the gypsy watching the bird gun firing into the colony of
>   seals; but it was filled with blanks;
> The face of the old knoll watching his hills grow up before him;
> The face of the New England fruit juice proprietor watching his whole
>   supplies being overturned by a herd of wild bulls;
> The face of a lemur watching the other primates become more
>   developed;
> The face of gold, as the entire world goes on the silver standard, but
>   gold remains extremely valuable and is the basis for international
>   exchange;
> The face of the sky, as the air becomes increasingly filled with smoke
>   and planes;
> The face of the young girl painted as Saint Urbana by Perugino, whose
>   large silver eyes are focused on the green pomegranate held by a
>   baby (it is Jesus) in the same painting;
> The face of the sea after there has been a storm, and the face of the valley
> When the clouds have blown away and it is going to be a pleasant day
>   and the pencils come out for their picnic;
> The face of the clouds;
> The faces of the targets when all the arrows are sticking out of them,
>   like tongues;
> The faces of insects; the tiny black moustachioed ineptitude of a fly;
> The faces of the splinters on the orange crate;
> The face of the Depression, which shook up America's faith in her
>   economy so badly;
> The face of President Hoover during this event;
> The face of Popeye; the face of Agamemnon; the face of Ruth in the
>   Bible; the face of Georges Simenon;
> The face of the hornet; the face of the carnation; of the orchid; the face
>   of the roots of the elm tree;
> The face of the fruit juice stand proprietor in Hawaii—it is black and
>   lined
> With the years and the climate[. . .]
>
> [. . .] jewelry's faces; faces of firemen; the face of the bowling pin; the
>   rhubarb's face
> When it is growing with abandon; the remarkable face of the street,
>   with the people in it, each one speaking, there is such a roar;
> The hero of comedy's face, when everything is going well,

And the hippopotamus's face, when he finds he has been put in the
   wrong zoo, there is no water,
And so he rages, damply, against the summer's bars;
And the chicken's face when the thief has not succeeded in stealing
   him;
The leader of the orchestra's face when the music flies off as if by magic
   (the wind carrying it) and the beautiful valentine face
With gold hair—it is real, you can touch it—reminding me of you
[. . .]

Surprise is the aspect of Koch's poem that most appeals to kids—
that is, the faces are surprised, caught in predicaments, victims of
practical jokes, or about to undergo some kind of dramatic trans-
formation. But along with the slapstick, in children's imitations of
Koch we find moments of gravity and genuine beauty.

Faces

The face of the globe looking so sad
The face of the chair when Fatso sits down
The faces of gods are powerful
The faces of cops are always scared
Faces of animals who have been wounded
Faces of plants when they're dying and haven't had light or water or
   plant food
Happy faces of people with lots of money spending it all in every store
Excited faces of dogs running in the rain
Faces of ladies ready to have babies
Mean faces of men with deadly weapons
Tired faces of people working in big hot offices
Faces of women getting their hair done
Faces of people posing in a picture
Peaceful faces of people sleeping in comfortable beds
The faces of lawyers are so serious
The faces of hockey players are often broken
The faces of the blades are always on the cutting edge
The face of the light when it is turned off
My brother's face when he is punished
The sun looking down at this racist world
The face of a tree when its leaves are falling
The face of a door when it is slammed

The face of night when something bad is going to happen
The faces of parents when their children are taken away
The face of a father when his son is grown up
My father's face when I broke his watch
The face of a hungry man when he is given food
The faces of big-nosed people who are always in somebody else's
    business
The faces of blond people when they laugh
The face of a person when they receive money
The face of a ball hit by a bat
The face of a sandwich when you take a bite
The face of my mother when she sees my report card
The face of a can when it's being crushed
Faces of drapes when they're pulled together
The face of melting snow
The face of the pond when you jump into it
Faces of words as you read them
Faces of letters as you spell
Faces of numbers as you count
Faces of balls bouncing in and out of life
My mother's face of joy and happiness smiling down upon my face
Faces of people who smell to the high unreachable heavens
Faces of heroes who save us from destruction
The faces of skinny people falling in and out of clothes
Faces of rhythm coming down into the nation
Face of love bringing people close together
Numbers and letters facing a common boundary to form a word
Faces of pain waiting to weaken a heart
Faces of villains trying to steal what you have worked hard for
Good and evil faces ready to test you
Faces of human brains expanding with knowledge
The face of the clock when time stops
Face of the dictionary when there are only nasty words to say
The face of crime when you're doing time
Street-face—people going crazy with screwed-up faces
Faces of old people wrinkled like bulldogs
Sad faces of babies without milk
Paulette's cute tongue sticking out of her face in a W
Face of a polar bear waving a pair of underwear
Cute boy's faces peeking out of their hoods
Big fat chubby cheeks of overweight children who are the cause of
    much trouble

The face of war is never pretty
The face of death is never able to extinguish itself
The face of love is always coming out full-bloom
The face of the last line means the end
  —*Peter Martinez, Wednesday Williams, Shamika Pope, Paulette Grimes, Alexis Martinez, and Michelle Nunery, seventh grade*

Faces

The face of the river when it evaporates
The face of the sun blocked by the moon
The face of Mrs. Bremer when I start my motor
The face of the waterfall when it trickles backwards
The face of the giraffe with a giant onion ring around its neck
The face of the Persian kitten with its violet eyes glittering in a black attic
The face of an elephant when its trunk turns into a suitcase
The face of the drummer when a turkey gobbles up his drumsticks
The face of the belly dancer when you push her belly button and a door opens
The face of a poodle when the fire hydrant walks away
The face of a cobra egg when it's about to be scrambled
The face of the mule when it kicks a statue
The face of the hamburger when it's smothered with whipped cream
The faces of cats and dogs when it rains umbrellas
Alphabet soup when the letters fall into the soup
Windowface washed by Windexface
Radio face full blast
Bubble faces
Face of Liberty Bell cracked again by lightning
Confused faces of Christmas trees at Easter
Shoeface stepping on Bazooka Gumface
Your face filled with my sunburst kisses, blushing like a radish, mouth wrinkling, lips chapped, teeth chattering
The face of the ape drinking blood
The face of the lollipop licked by a steel tongue
The face of the bare foot slipping in a puddle of prune juice
The face of the speedboat sinking in boiling lava
Face of the grape rolling in a golf hole
The face of Rockefeller Center when Rockefeller gets hits by rocks and becomes just another feller
Potato face with false eyelashes

Mudface
Busface as it steers over Niagara Falls
The face of the alligator with a teacher stuck in its jaws
That teacher's face
Ropeface wrapped around neckface
Faces of people after you've shaved your head
The face of someone finding half a worm in their apple
The face of a cross-eyed mule sucking on a lollipop
The face of someone who just threw out the winning lottery ticket
The face of the girl who gets pushed into a crowded boys' bathroom
The face of the sleepwalker who wakes up in the wrong house
The face of the sergeant when he throws the pin instead of the grenade
The face of "about" when the sergeant calls it
The face of the Easter Bunny when the chickens go on strike
The face of Edmund Hillary when he found a camper waiting for him
    on top of Mt. Everest
The face of a face looking in the mirror at a completely different face
The face of Raquel Welch when she gains a pound
The face of a pound when it finds itself on Raquel Welch's body
The face of the clock as it ticks off the last seconds in the life of a face
Computer face—digit eyes
Best face of 1974—my face
    —Sixth and seventh grade group

Keeping the same general format, but limiting the topic to eyes, yields a blend as rich as faces or whole bodies. Here, the puns and metaphors are less complex and clever, the lines more spontaneous, romantic, surrealistic.

Your Eyes

With your eyes like skulls that grin in a dark corner
With your eyes like hearts that bump away on your funny face
With your eyes like pennies that turn blue and purple
With your eyes like moons that yawn at dawn
With your eyes like cotton balls that sleep all day
With your eyes like butterflies fluttering under your eyebrows
With your eyes like apples that creep on the floor at night
With your eyes like asteroids that explore the earth
With your eyes like peaches that crunch when you blink
With your eyes like clocks that tick when you see a pretty lady
With your eyes like hearts that pump when you kiss

With your eyes like marbles sparkling in the evening
With your eyes like tables of leather
With your eyes like calendars of wool
With your eyes like pearls that sing you to sleep
With your eyes like shining stars that raise children who are born to be
        good
With your eyes like pennies that rust in cold water
With your eyes like bells shaking with tones of music
With your eyes like buttons that you wear like pearls in the air that
        looks like a cloud
With your eyes like owls' heads—I wouldn't touch them! I wouldn't
        touch them at all!
With your eyes like black olives rolling across the desert
With your eyes like ice-cream cones that make you boogie
With your eyes like spongeballs squirting cream soda
With your eyes like bees buzzing your temper to outer space
With your eyes like rings of fire that circus lions jump through
With your yo-yo eyes that snap back and explode
With your eyes like footballs flying in the Cotton Bowl
With your eyes like skulls of mice
Tiny mirrors
Slimy erasers
Diamonds of the moon
Hearts breaking in your head!
Suns that make your hair shine!
Eyes like crystal balls that act like boxing gloves
With your eyes like balloons that take you up
        —*Third and fourth grade group*

Eyes

The eyes of the sky when it's looking over everybody's shoulders
The eyes of the pencil as it reads along with every word it writes
The eyes of gum, blinded by grinding teeth
The eyes of the walls when they close in on you in your tiny chair
Temperature eyes rising
Gold brick eyes shining in the beady vault
Eyes of the teacher scanning the room for naughty children, like blips
        on a radar screen
Turtle eyes
Innocent blinking eyes of a child with a chocolate milk mustache
Peaceful cow eyes in a shiny green meadow

The sleepy eyes of the mountains with cloudy eyebrows
Eyes of red beads on a white throat
Melting jellybean eyes
Eyes of leaves drifting from the branches with caterpillar eyebrows
 wiggling like Groucho Marx
Dot eyes connecting to make the wrinkled eyes of an old woman,
 rocking and rolling
Mommy's eyes watering over the eyes of the onions
Crying eyes of the young girl—she won't have a Christmas
Eyes of stone—angry with everyone
Marshmallow eyes of powdery kindness
 —*Diane Ospina, Elizabeth Lourenso, and Pamela Nardi,*
 eighth grade

Chapter 6

Things to Do

Besides shopping lists, many of us jot down reminders—lists of things to do during the course of the day or week, from practical necessities to frivolous pleasures and anything in between. When traveling, we make a list of things to do and see on our visit.

Gary Snyder was perhaps the first to write a *Things to Do* poem. His are like guided minitours of cities, with a personal twist—details of Snyder's life in these places.

Things to Do around Portland

Go walk along the Sandy when the smelt run
Drink Buttermilk at the Buttermilk Corner.
Walking over Hawthorne Bridge the car tires sing
Take the trolley out to Sellwood when cherries are in bloom.
Hiking the woods below Council Crest, a treehouse high in a Douglas
    fir near the medical school.
Bird watching and plant hunting on Sauvies Island in May.
Vine maple leaves in the slopes above St. John's Bridge in autumn.
Wading the Columbia out to sandbars
Himalayan blackberries tangle at the base of steel high-tension Bonneville
    transmission tower
                    your fingers staind—
Get married in Vancouver, without the three-day wait.
Cash paychecks at the Pastime
Beer in Ericson's, hamburgers at
    Tic Tock.
Led down narrow corridors of Court House, City Hall, the newspapers,
    the radios, the jail
Parking in the Park blocks
Sunburned skiing
Shivering at the ocean
Standing in the rain

Things to Do around San Francisco

Catch eels in the rocks below the Palace of the Legion of Honor.
Four in the morning—congee at Sam Wo.
Walk up and down Market, upstairs playing pool,
Turn on at Aquatic Park—seagulls steal bait-sardine
Going clear out to Oh's to buy bulghour.
Howard Street Goodwill—
Not paying traffic tickets; stopping the phone.
Merry-go-round at the beach, the walk up to the cliff-house, sea-lions
    and tourists—the old washed out road that goes on—
Play chess at Mechanics'

Dress up and go looking for work,
Seek out the Wu-t'ung trees, park arboretum.
Suck in the sea air and hold it;
    miles of white walls
    sunset shoots back from somebody's window
    high in the Piedmont hills
Get drunk all the time. Go someplace and score.
Walk in and walk out of the Asp
Walk up Tam
Keep quitting and starting at Berkeley
Watch the Pike in the Steiner Aquarium:
                he doesn't move.
Sleeping with strangers
Keeping up on the news
Chanting sutras after sitting
Practising yr frailing on guitar;

Get dropped off in the fog in the night
Fall in love twenty times
Get divorced
Keep moving—move out to the Sunset—
Get lost   or
Get found

In Ted Berrigan's *Things to Do* poems there are touches similar
to Snyder's, but the progression is more diffuse, the tone romanti-
cally urgent.

Things to Do in New York City
for Peter Schjeldahl

Wake up high up
            frame bent & turned on
Moving slowly
            & by the numbers
light cigarette
Dress in basic black
            & reading a lovely old man's book:

BY THE WATERS OF MANHATTAN

change

            flashback

play cribbage on the Williamsburg Bridge
watching the boats sail by
the sun, like a monument
move slowly up the sky
above the bloody rush:

break yr legs & break yr heart
kiss the girls & make them cry
loving the gods & seeing them die

            celebrate your own
            & everyone else's birth:

            Make friends forever
            & go away

"Anne's Room" is a lot smaller than New York, but Berrigan
finds enough to do there.

Things to Do in Anne's Room

Walk right in
            sit right down
                        baby, let your hair hang down

87

It's on my face that hair
& I'm amazed to be here
the sky outside is green the blue
shows thru the trees

I'm on my knees

     unlace Li'l Abner
   shoes
       place them under the bed
           light cigarette
  study out the dusty bookshelves,

                          sweat

Now I'm going to do it

     SELF RELIANCE
     THE ARMED CRITIC
     MOBY DICK
     THE WORLD OF SEX
     THE PLANET OF THE APES

Now I'm going to do it

   deliberately

              take off clothes
       shirt goes on the chair
       pants go on the shirt
       socks next to shoes next to bed

       the chair goes next to the bed

       get into the bed
       be alone
       suffocate
       don't die

         & it's that easy

Given the adult nature of the examples above, I don't use them as models in the classroom. Instead I tailor the general notion of *Things to Do* to suit the students I'm working with, as in the following examples.

Things to Do in Kindergarten

join the circle
listen to the stories
show & tell
have a snack
color
talk into the recorder
play an instrument
say the magic word
     —Kindergarten group

Things to Do besides Drugs

Learn a trade
Have fun with your family
Travel
Read
Write a book
Finish school
Surf
Sail
Skate
Get a job
Talk to your best friend
See counsellors
Sing and dance
     —Shiba Perry, Lightbourne Dyer, O'Shea Hunter, Glen Delamota, Joy Robinson, and Sophie Lewis, seventh and eighth grades

An interesting variation on the assignment, with more psychological clout:

Things I'd Like to Do but Am Afraid To

Stick my hand in a fan, touch a snake, copy a dollar bill, walk on the train tracks, ride a motorbike, take my TV apart, parachute off the Statue of Liberty, hang-glide off the Twin Towers, climb Mount Everest, get all my hair shaved off, grow an Afro, go an entire year without getting a haircut, race in the Indy 500, teach (but I don't know anything), be a cop (but I'm not that dumb), eat sushi, sky dive (without throwing up), have a party in school (no teachers), cut every strand of hair off my body, touch a bear, be a troublemaker, go to sleep in first period class, burn all the pink slips, go on stage and sing, beat up my uncle, stand up on the roller-coaster, feel what it's like to be shot, dress a dead person, kiss my aunt, hit a girl with a "built" father, stay out till 3 A.M., use a chainsaw, cut school, kick a pit bull, talk to someone I like, explore space, marry, eat a big spoon of hot noodles in one swallow, break all the answering machines, play one-on-one with Magic Johnson, fight Mike Tyson, buy a dog for my mother, get a job without permission, cut off my arm and get a robotic one, swim in the ocean, be the class clown, go to Los Angeles, see a tiger from the inside.

—Seventh grade class

Chapter 7

Lining Up My Toys
(List Poems about Being Alone)

I've always marveled at the ability of kids to write creatively, "under the gun," in a crowded classroom. Try it sometime, if you haven't already. We think of solitude as a requirement for the creative act or, indeed, for concentration on any intensive mental task. Poetry has been called "the sullen art"—sullen in its original meaning of *solitary, alone.* But being alone doesn't necessarily mean being lonely, sad, or frightened, as some people would claim. The poet Marianne Moore once declared that the best remedy for loneliness is solitude.

I ask the kids how they feel and what they do when they're alone. Some of us become restless, nervous, our minds wander; others are single-minded, intent on some purposeful mental or physical activity; still others become vegetative. We reflect, remember, wonder, fantasize, daydream, talk to ourselves or to an imaginary friend. We clean, cook, eat, bathe, nap. We listen to music or dance to it, solo. We rest, listening to silence or the neighbors. We play an instrument, draw, or write—letters, journals, poems, stories, or even lists (like this one). If we wander around the house stark naked or wearing a funny hat, it's nobody's business but our own. I don't believe that talking on the phone, watching television, or enjoying the company of a pet count as being alone. After I discuss these ideas with my students, and when I feel they are "primed" for the assignment, I have them write.

> When I'm alone I get scared because I think the hammer man will
> come and take me.
> When I'm alone, I get happy because I could do anything I want.
> Not anything, but anything.
> —*Cesar Mercedes, fourth grade*

> When I'm alone I'm not afraid.
> I have the television.
> I have myself.
> —*Anibal Vasquez, fourth grade*

When I'm alone I don't daydream, I simply go to the Nintendo.
When I'm alone the mission is impossible.
I take care of the house.
The mission is complete.
        —*Edwin Figueroa, fourth grade*

When I'm alone I cook rice and pork chops.
When I'm alone I feel like cleaning the whole house just to see it clean.
I don't like to see a dirty house.
        —*Carmen Nieves, fourth grade*

When I'm alone I put on some music and try to dance like The Joker.
When I'm alone I take my mother's towels and tie them to the high
        drawer and try to act like Indiana Jones.
I make believe my pillows are the bad guys.
        —*Robert Santiago, fourth grade*

When I'm alone I fight Ninjas.
When I'm alone I play with my hamsters.
When I'm alone I wrestle with my cushion.
When I'm alone I get so bored I draw weird looking people.
        —*Tony Brown, sixth grade*

When I'm alone I eat and eat and eat and eat.
When I'm alone I feel like I am a strange girl.
When I'm alone I like to lie on my bed and make shadows with my
        fingers.
        —*Lisandra Rodriguez, sixth grade*

When I'm alone I hit myself.
When I'm alone I say "Should I or should I not?"
When I'm alone I jump on an old mattress.
When I'm alone there's nothing to worry about any more.
I wander around in a circle saying, "I am alone."
        —*Leslie Misla, sixth grade*

When I'm alone I sometimes read in the silent air.
When I'm alone I worry about what will happen in the near future.
When I'm alone I think of doing things but I don't because I don't have
        anyone to do it with.
When I'm alone I sometimes feel like going to my sister's room and
        messing all her things up.
When I'm alone my mind goes empty like a box.
        —*Peter Cleary, sixth grade*

When I'm alone I start to cry because I remember my imaginary friend
died.
When I'm alone I play Monopoly with my teddy bear.
When I'm alone I draw a monster called Margaret the Frog on the wall.
    —*Margaret Johnson, sixth grade*

A collaborative poem about solitude may seem like a contra-
diction. In fact such a poem is different from one written individually,
it is more various and spacious, but usually less poignant.

When I'm alone I wander around doing nothing.
When I'm alone I cook soup.
When I'm alone I remember my granddaddy talking to me and telling
    me he loves me.
When I'm alone I draw pictures then I get very anxious.
When I'm alone I talk to myself and say, "Carmen, why do you goof
    off so much?"
When I'm alone I think about my family and start to cry.
When I'm alone I feel strange.
When I'm alone I imagine that I'm a queen.
When I'm alone I write about monsters.
When I'm alone I eat a lot of cookies.
I feel like writing in my diary about what happened today.
I can hear the silence around me, it is all calm.
I imagine I am in a crowded but lonely place.
When I'm alone I remember the bad times.
When I'm alone I think someone will break into my house.
When I'm alone I feel relieved because my little sister isn't there to
    disturb me.
I feel relieved from danger because my little sister will do anything to
    make my hair short like cut it all off so I can be bald.
When I'm bored I go into the kitchen and make a mess.
I spilled flour all over my black and white suit.
I washed the chicken off and rubbed it into the powder.
Then I ate me a donut.
There was a moment of silence and quiet. It was nice and then I got
    worried about when I was going to see my mother because she
    went shopping.
When I'm alone I dream that I was the richest girl in the world, that
    I had anything I wanted. My mother walked in the door and woke
    me up. I said, "Ma, I have a feeling that I want a little green stuff."
    So she gave me five bucks.

When I'm alone I have a favorite pillow that I lie on. It makes me feel better.

When I'm alone I feel frightened because it is like being in a dark corner.

When I'm alone I am anxious to know what everybody's doing.

When I'm alone I like to draw wedding dresses or write songs.

When I'm alone I feel like I'm the only person living on the earth.

When I'm alone everything is black and not a soul moves or makes a sound.

Sometimes I wander in my own world and begin to play with my fingers.

When I'm alone sometimes I study and when I'm not I don't!

When I'm alone I throw water balloons out the window.

  —*Sixth grade class*

Alone

I'm alone in the night
When I'm alone I'm relieved
I imagine sounds, things, or anything
I think, Is there a monster?
Alone is frightening
Thoughts and thoughts pass through my mind
I even talk to myself, to my wall
Sometimes I write and write until my hands get so tired
I can't lift anything
Silence is beautiful when you are alone
Questions and sadness is everything in your mind
Happiness is not so great
Sadness is just there when you need it
It is a feeling that any human animal feels
An emptiness in your heart
Time is not important when you're alone
It doesn't matter if it's going fast or slow
You just wonder
Wonder about your body, the sky, the moon, the earth, space, your boyfriend
What he's thinking about now and why
Who was the first person on earth
You just wonder
Sometimes you even get curious about
How we dream, how we cry, how we write

You just get curious
About yourself
And everything around you.
  —*Yudelka Fernandez, seventh grade*

Alone

When I am alone
I hear the clock tick
I hear the water
Dripping in the sink

I imagine I am a spy
I imagine I am being taught karate
I imagine that I am someone—
A famous person

I feel happy that I'm alone
I feel happy that there is no one else
I feel happy that no one
Is calling me

It feels like I want to scream
It feels like time is flying
It feels like time is frozen
When I am alone

I daydream that I am somewhere else
I daydream that I am the mayor
I daydream about someone I like
I daydream about something special

I'm very bored
I want something to do
It's quiet
I hear the clock ticking

I think about what I can do
I think about what is outside
I think about what I can do
Tonight
  —*Anthony Smith, seventh grade*

When I'm Alone

When I'm alone my life changes
When I'm alone I feel sadness
When I'm alone my tears come down
When I'm alone my brain is empty
When I'm alone I'm silent
I hate the darkness
I lie down and think
I think I might cry more
I think quietly
I feel sorry about some things I do in life
When I am alone I hate myself
When I am alone strange sounds are floating
I am alone in my bed
I worry about my life
Nobody feels sorry for me
I am thinking of my family
My mind is calm
My heart is beating
I see the stars and the moon
I hate people who are fighting
My closet is empty
My tears go into my mouth
My life is ruined
I'm always sitting in a chair thinking about my puppy
I am depressed that my puppy died
Life is hard
I feel sorry for the world
When I'm alone I am the king
My doll cries and I get up and walk to make her stop
Feelings are everywhere, my doll has them too
When I am alone I line up my toys
I feel my life passing before my eyes
I got a life
It is boring
    —Second grade group

Although being alone at *night* can be more lonely and frightening, especially for a child, I try, when assigning a night poem, to prevent kids from going overboard with scary images, nightmares, etc. First we brainstorm about night: darkness and light, night animals, sounds and shapes, thoughts and emotions, falling asleep and dreaming. I ask the kids for descriptions of their rooms and what's right outside in the neighborhood.

Here's a fourth grade brainstorm sheet—a list of night words to work with:

pajamas	moon	peace	robbers
bed	stars	sleep	prayers
blankets	trees	dream	teddy bear
sheets	branches	nightmare	dolls
pillow	owls	ghost	rain
closet	crickets	cars	midnight snack
lamp	cats	trucks	refrigerator
radio	mice	lonely	planes
flashlight	silence	sad	shadows
curtains	nervous	ticking	romantic
window	afraid	clock	candlelight
wind	footsteps	voices	breeze
snoring	creeping		

And here, using poet Dick Gallup's format of "In the middle of the night" to start each line, is one result:

In the Middle of the Night

In the middle of the night coyotes howl
In the middle of the night I blew my nose
In the middle of the night I get ants in my pants
Ghosts moan and chains rattle
Dracula sucks my blood
I'm hungry
I sneak cupcakes and roast beef
In the middle of the night I wake up and stay up
I'm burning up in the middle of the night
I shout hello
Police arrest ghost robbers
Watchdogs stare at the sky
In the middle of the hospital ugly nurses scare patients out of their skins
In the middle of the night my hair starts to itch
In the middle of the night I take ten aspirin
I turn into a chicken

My hair pops up
In the middle of the night a shooting star makes a glazed red line in the
    sky
In the middle of the night I get in-di-GES-tion
In the middle of the night I see hands crawling on the floor
I step on them
    —*Fourth grade class*

In the night I sleep like a pig.
In the night I dream the pig goes to heaven.
In the night I see stars twinkling in the window.
In the night the moon is spinning like a crystal ball.
In the night my pajamas glow in the dark.
In the night the darkness glows like the inside of a cave.
In the night the breeze blows hard on my silent pajamas.
In the night the ghost of the living dead smiles at my baby doll.
In the night all my dolls wave at the ghosts.
In the night I dream of living crickets who crawl inside my pajamas.
In the night my shy little baby sleeps his head off.
In the night owls hoot to the glaring sky.
In the night pickles whisper to 7-Up.
In the night my heart beats slowly and quietly like the only muscle I
    have.
In the night soft jazz plays into the windy darkness.
In the night fog clouds up the land.
In the night the river sleeps and dreams about the magic flounder.
In the night the kingfish grounds me for nothing.
In the night the little mermaid shakes her tail and finds her prince.
In the night the clothes in the hamper are exhausted.
In the night time does not sleep.
In the night the closet silently opens.
In the night I lie awake thinking about Fred.
In the night my butler wakes me for a joke.
In the night the janitor gently sweeps the school.
In the night Mrs. Dixon heats up the milk for the baby.
    —*Dana Lespinasse, Jose Guerrido, and Jerry Raphael,*
    second grade

In the night my pajamas ripped off in the breeze.
In the night a pink ghost drove to the cemetery.
In the night I ate four jellybeans.
In the night my eyes pop open when I hear a snow owl feeding her
    babies.

In the night my dolls grabbed my bowl of Froot Loops.
In the night bubbles of Miss Piggy swayed over the sea.
In the night my barrettes scratch my head.
In the night my underwear danced through the sleeping home.
In the night the moon came out and up and down and rolled around
    like a lighted bowl.
In the night the stars sparkled like a glittery dress of snowy eyes.
In the night car lights slid through my walls.
In the night Donahue whispered into my ear.
In the night my teeth glow like gorgeous flowers.
In the night my blankets turn into little shortcakes.
In the night my sheets wrap around my head like a fireball.
In the night my mother goes to the bathroom.
I am not afraid of staying alone.
In the night I have faith in my father.
In the night the quiet deadness filled a truck.
In the night flowers faint and die.
In the night seven ghosts visited the bathroom and ran into my mother.
In the night I crawl in bed with a spider.
In the night scissors of glue clip and clip.
In the night my sister sticks my feet with toothpicks.
In the night I tapdance in front of Sammy Davis, Jr.
In the night the peaceful ballet came into my dressing room.
In the night the clouds cannot leave the room.
In the night the river carries many frogs.
    —*Kelvin Moncayo, Candice Robinson, and Ananie Noel,*
    second grade

Night

No wind is as cold as tonight
No dark is as dark as tonight
No street is as empty as tonight
Because my heart is as sad as tonight
    —*Lok Man Kwong, eighth grade*

In the night I can hear the crickets chirping and chirping
Sometimes I count how many times they chirp
To see if I can fall asleep
In the night I hear my brother open the refrigerator
And the light shines under my door crack
In the night it is so dark I can't even see myself

I think my body isn't here
In the night I say to myself my bed is so comfortable
But I don't want to go to sleep
In the night it is so silent I can hear the bed squeak
And the wind blow, though my windows are closed
In the night my grandmother snores as she falls asleep
In the night I do not hear gunshots
My block is a quiet block
Neat and clean
In the night the dim light of the moon
Reflects on my window
Then I fall asleep
Knowing the moon is there with me
        —*Vanessa Cardenas, seventh grade*

In the Night

In the night I hear a sound
It is an owl and a cricket
Making a beautiful night song

In the night I feel romantic
I try to compose music
On my keyboard

In the night I am surprised
I see a shooting star
And wish upon it

In the night I wake up
I hear a silence
A total silence

In the night I look out the window
The moon is staring
At me

In the night I feel
Only the space
Between me and the sky

Sadness on the moon's face
Shadows on the stars
I feel scared

I wonder and wonder
How God made the earth
Stars, moon, sky, space

In the night my dreams
Become realities
My nightmares become tears

In the night I snuggle
With my teddy bear
My only friend is my bed

In the night something
Wakes me up
I look around my room
—*Yudelka Fernandez, seventh grade*

In the Night

In the night I hear a knock on the door but it's only my little Jemimah
I was only doing nothing but looking out my window
What such pretty stars!
How they are sparkling!
I had on my silk pajamas
And how the air came through!
My little sister left the room
How good it feels to be alone
In the darkness of the night
I lay my sleepy head on my cool pillow
The stars light my open window
My curtains go up and down
I can hear the crickets chirping
Then a big man with a face of worms says GET OUT!
But I stay
Each times he comes with a different face
But I stay
An owl hoots
The shadow of a goat is in my room

My mother sleepwalks into the light
I think she's a wolf
The owl sits in my window
Shooting stars sparkle over my bed
I see black clouds
The moon goes down
Shadows of the cars roll by
The ground is damp
I am so quiet
>—*Shameeka Upshaw, Gregory Hamberry, Winnie Burgess, Erik*
>*Gonzagne, Lukeman Ogunyinka, Ronald Peterson, Ebony*
>*Gallashaw, Sheena Walker, Clarissa Roberts, Edwin Negron,*
>*Jemimah Peter, and Angela Rivera, fourth grade*

There's quite a range of moods here, from the raucous and capricious to the eloquent and sensitive. The tone of the writing is usually determined by the tone of the brainstorming. Sometimes even the topic can veer off and become something else. This happened once when a fifth grade group was brainstorming *night* and got sidetracked into *darkness* alone. They wrote about dark places.

Darkness

Mr. Boogie came out of the closet.
Inside my mouth it's hot and dark.
Under my bed where my shoes live.
It's pitch black in my shoes.
A turtle's shell without the turtle.
In the garbage can.
Out in the galaxy.
Inside the faucet.
In the cabinets and wine bottles.
In a closed book.
In a box.
Under the covers.
In a wolf's stomach.
Inside a whale egg.
Up in the attic, down in the cellar.
Bottom of the ocean.
Inside the *Titanic*.
In a kangaroo's pouch.

In my mind when I'm alone.
Blackout.
Nightmare.
In a corner.
In the alley.
Fog.
Coffin.

Back on track, we can easily segue from night to:

Morning

I open my eyes
I stare into my pillow
A bright light shines on my cheek
I stretch
I yawn
I push back the covers
I swing my legs out of bed
I go to the bathroom
I look at my face
I see a mess
I begin to straighten it out
I wash my hands and face
I scrub my skin
I do my hair
With a comb
With a brush
With my gel
With DAX
I brush my teeth
I put on my clothes
My shirt
My skirt
My jeans
My hat
My many shoes
My silver
My gold
My diamonds
My pearls
My glitter

My Cardinals cap
My eyeshadow
The sun glares in the window
The whole house is bright
The walls are yellow and warm
I go to the kitchen
I fill up a bowl with Cheerios and milk
I eat an egg
I swallow coffee
I butter a muffin
I grab my books
I'm out the door
I walk along
I begin to wake up

    *—Adrianne Davis, Amanda Raysor, Serita Hall, Joesian
    Denizard, Francine Laurel, and José Liriano, sixth and
    seventh grades*

Chapter 8

I Went Out With Vanessa del Rio (Using Kenneth Koch's Teaching Ideas)

Wishes, Lies, and Dreams, Kenneth Koch's inspiring book about teaching children how to write poetry, has been a faithful and useful companion throughout my years as a visiting writer in the schools. As Koch points out, children are rarely given the chance in school to express themselves on secret or fantastical matters. When encouraged to delve into the mind's hidden recesses, they can come up with startlingly fresh material. Quite a few of the poems in *Wishes, Lies, and Dreams* are list poems.

There are many subcategories of wishes: wishing for things for yourself, or for others; wishing for special powers or abilities; for good things to happen in the world; for bad things to disappear; for something to turn into something else. All of these are reflected in these examples:

> I wish I had an ape that would beat the men in the bank and steal all
>   the money.
> I wish I was 2,000,000 years old.
> I wish I had a young skunk.
> I would walk down the street with my little skunk and terrify the
>   population.
> I wish that my sisters would go away.
> And stay away.
> *—Danny Corcoran, sixth grade*

> I wish I was the owner of the Earth and could make Asia and Africa
>   come together.
> I wish I could turn New York into a big store.
> In the store would be stuff you never dreamed of, and it would be free
>   for kids of all nations!
> I wish I could fly a jet to any place I wanted.
> *—Steven Kaplan, sixth grade*

I wish I was a kangaroo.
I wish I was a garbage pail.
I wish I was trash.
I wish I was a scissors so I could cut someone.
I wish I was a super.
I wish I was a card.
I wish I was Spider Girl.
I wish I was a blood-red and golden book.
I wish I was a bee-bee.
I wish I was the letter "I."
I wish I had one eye.
I wish I was a gooey monster.
I wish I was 15.
I wish I had a babysitter.
I wish I was a penguin.
I wish I was a shining light.
I wish I was Dick Grayson.
I wish I was a wishbone.
I wish I was a paper and be torn.
I wish I was a dead duck.
    —*Third grade group*

I wish my dog would have kittens and my snake would have puppies.
I wish it would snow forever.
I wish my cousin would go on vacation.
I wish I were an orange clown.
I wish the President would let me on the Great Adventure.
    —*Steve Mills, fourth grade*

I wish my pillow was a giant marshmallow.
I wish I had ten giant eyes.
I wish the school would close forever.
I wish the wars would fade away.
I wish I knew what everybody else was wishing.
I wish I didn't have to write this.
    —*Bill McShane, fifth grade*

I wish I were eating 20 apples.
I wish I were a cloud.
I wish you were nice.
I wish the class respected the teacher.
I wish I could do my own hair.

I wish I could read good.
I wish I could ice skate.
I wish I could tell time.
I wish I could help people out at work.
I wish I had a frog to scare the class.
I wish people would like me.
I wish I had 1,000 puppies.
I wish I had a little quiet and soft cat.
I wish I had a garden.
I wish the world were nice and cool.
I wish the people in this world were nice and sweet and generous and
    kind and helpful.
I wish I were in Oklahoma.
I wish I had a house.
I wish I had a baby sister.
I wish I would never see people use drugs.
I wish everyone would respect each other.
I wish President Bush were alive.
I wish my sister would stop hitting me.
I wish I were a man.
I wish I went to a nice show.
I wish I could believe mom.
I wish I could see what's in space.
I wish I were God.
I wish I had a gold house full of money.
I wish nobody would die in 1990 for real.
I wish I lived in a pretty hotel.
I wish the whole world would share brotherhood.
I wish I had a big fat pit bull.
I wish my baby cousin would get bigger.
I wish the army wouldn't use my father just for fun.
I wish I had a son.
I wish I were a plant.
    —*Second grade group*

•

When Kenneth Koch used the word *lie* in his book, he was not
encouraging dishonesty, but rather invention and imagination. The
excitement of exaggerating or making up untrue or unreal things is
infectious, and the list poem is a perfect form for these fantasies. As

the list grows, the lies are compounded. But there is also some truth mixed in, and some lies that paradoxically are true.

Lies

I stayed up all night.
I got swallowed by a crocodile.
I made the world upsidedown and then
I made everything upsidedown and then
The people and the grass was on top of them
And a house.
The lion was going to bite one and
I took a magnifying glass
And made myself big.
He fell in the hot water
And I fell in with him.
I was caught by an octopus
In the Empire State Building.
I went up to the moon in a big rocket ship
And when I got up to the moon
It was just a round little circle.
It wasn't as big as I thought.
I don't know what to say.
I went under the water and got bit by a shark.
I went out to the moon and found
A great big dinosaur.
I hate working in school.
You don't know anything.
I hate my teachers because they're yelling
At me and stuff.
Our teacher hits us with a ruler
And she really hits hard.
She hits us on your back.
My father got a truck and goes to work.
Daddy works at an ugly house.
My daddy works in the North Pole.
Dwight, my brother, he plays in church.
He works like in government.
He works stupid.
My father tells the biggest lies.
My father skates on ice skates.

My father earns a lot of money.
My arms don't have no bones at all
Or no blood.
My father can't hear.
I'm skinny and don't have no bones.
My father is a big fat man.
I had a balloon and went up into the air.
I was on the telephone and he cut me off.
I was in a car and my car flew up in the air.
I took my car to work and crashed into a wall.
I have a car and I am just 3 years old.
I drove a car in a theater.
The theater is a movie.
I chiseled the wall and I made a sun
And the next morning I woke up
And it was in real life.
I took off in the air.
Someone picked my fingers off.
My fingers came all off with my arms.
I had a hot dog and it was still barking.
I made a house and I made it ugly and then
I lived in it.
—*Trevor Oestricher, Octavia Oestricher, and Didi Critchlow, second grade*

Remember Ripley's *Believe It or Not?* I passed out xeroxes from it to serve as models for this wacko pack of lies:

Believe It or Not

The Queen of America looks like the devil!
The Skeleton Tribe of Danger Island has NO SKIN. Paper is glued to
    their bones!
A rat with 4 eyeballs can see a cat with 10 toes 40 miles away!
The Finger Brothers of Chicago have 34 fingers between them!
They play grand piano!
    —*Fifth grade group*

And here's another variation on the "lie" theme, this one with rhymes and a snappy refrain:

Wanna Make a Bet?

I saw a chicken smoke a pipe
Wanna make a bet?
I saw a steel tomato but it wasn't ripe
Wanna make a bet?
I am Diana Ross
Wanna make a bet?
My nose is covered with moss
Wanna make a bet?
New York is an animal
Wanna make a bet?
A fly is a mammal
Wanna make a bet?
My dog can spin wheat into gold
Wanna make a bet?
My entire block was sold
Wanna make a bet?
My sister kissed a monkey
Wanna make a bet?
I'm in love with a donkey
Wanna make a bet?
Tarzan is in the shower
Wanna make a bet?
Pee Wee Herman lives in a tower
Wanna make a bet?
  —Third and fourth grade group

This next group contains some hybrids—combinations of "lies"
and secret truths revealed:

Things I'll Never Tell You

When I was 8 I drank a bottle of gin and danced in front of my mother
She didn't know anything
I pray she'll never know
One day I put my cat in the dryer
And my cat was french toast
I ate a fish from my fish tank
I have a deformed tongue
I was scared to get it clipped
I used to think you could break into the TV and take the toys out

I used to be scared of using the toilet because I thought it was filled
With alligators
I am Julius Caesar
I will kill Brutus and bury him in the garage
I used to think that if I fell off a cliff in a dream I would die
I threw an egg out the window
And hit a housing man on the leg
He caught me and put me in the hammerlock
And made me recite the 11th Commandment:
Thou Shalt Not Throw Eggs
I'll never tell you that when I was small I'd wake up my grandparents
So they could come with me to the bathroom at night
When I babysit a child I hit them every little time they do some-thing
When I threw my brother out the window he landed in a pile of
    garbage
I knocked out Mike Tyson
I put thumbtacks in my aunt's bed
A Halloween mask got stuck on my face
I burned my butt on the radiator
I got stuck in the toilet
Freddy slashed me across my face
I used to cry over everything
I'm scared of needles
I've never been in an airplane
My friend Shamika was a bum and I bought her all the clothes she has
I got chased by a rat all the way to my doorstep
I tricked you into eating dog food when you asked for chili
My dog eats carrots
I used to fly a plane but I blew up the Stealth bomber and they fired
    me
I used to help my neighbors with their bags
And take them to my house instead of theirs
    —*Seventh grade group*

I superglued your dog to the floor
And repeatedly smacked it after it bit me
I found out you were bald
When you thought you had your wig on
I got undressed and ran out of the building in the middle of the day
I sneezed my brains out my nose
I'll never tell you about the flattop under my arms
I can walk on water

I went out with Vanessa Del Rio
She was too much
I'll never tell you I got hit by a swing
I bought Marcus a whole box of peppermints
A bird walked up to me and said, "Don't throw those away, give them
   to me!"
I have a crush on a girl in my 7th grade class
I cursed at a teacher once
I used to stand on my head on the couch every day
I was the dumbest kid in the class
I used to cry myself to sleep every night
I'll never tell you that I never told anyone that I never broke my
   mother's fan
When I got on an airplane I thought my ears were going to pop off
I thought I'd see God in the sky
I thought my cat could talk but she was too shy
I took all my sister's panties and flushed them down the toilet
I had a friend who had no hair
But she had a comb and brush set
I had a dog named James Boone
I thought books read to you
I don't like you
I have a chipped tooth
I kissed my second cousin
I used to think if I ate too much I would blow up
I have eaten dirt before
My dog is afraid of paper bags
I used to think when it rained God was crying
I used to think you could buy babies
I took my mother's bank card
I thought my fan was a blender
I put bleach in my sister's food
I am scared of elevators
Donald is my cousin but we don't want anyone to know we're related
A dog tried to bite me but I bit it back
I wear fake gold
At night I saw big spiders and turtles coming out of my closet
I used to believe in Santa Claus—he was Jewish
When I was upside down on a roller coaster I thought my insides would
   come out through my head
I thought they named people after animals
I thought Magic Johnson was a magician

I dream about girls every day
I have imaginary friends named Tom, Dick, and Harry
I'm shy around girls
I'm scared of liver
I stole two vanilla cupcakes from the supermarket
   —*Seventh grade group*

Below, in "I Never Told Anybody" (the title of another Koch book), the kids tell true secrets about themselves with a kind of sheepish grin. They are confessions about little embarrassments and peccadillos, kids tattling on themselves.

I Never Told Anybody

I never told anybody but
I thought there were people in radios and I would talk in the antenna
   and ask them to play a song I liked.
I never told anybody but
I once saved a gingerbread man's head from going under the guillotine
   and getting chopped off.
I used to say "waw waw" when it was water.
I used to always cry to get out of messes.
Whenever I would pour the milk into the Rice Krispies cereal I
   thought that little radios made the sounds.
I never told anybody but
I have glasses and I have to wear them but I don't.
I used to think my dolls would eat me alive.
When I was in second grade I had lots of girlfriends.
I never told anybody
But when I saw Xmas I thought they were cancelling Christmas.
I used to think the moon was following me.
I thought George Washington was a city.
I always used to eat the shell with the peanut.
I never told anybody but
When I was little I used to hide from the sun.
I threw oatmeal on my mother's head. (I was only three years old.)
I thought no one loved me.
I thought if I got into the tub I would drown.
I never told anybody but
I love the dark.

I love the girls in my class.
I used to be very shy.
I thought that people got their names from books.
I never told anybody but
When I was little and I was watching TV I shut it off and thought the
    movie would stop till I came back.
I never told anybody but
I once made an eraser fall out the window.
I never told anybody but
I still believe in Santa!
    —*Fifth and sixth grade group*

A kind of cross between wishing and dreaming is the *If I Were/
I Would* poem:

If I were a scissors I would make a squeaky noise and cut me a circle.
If I were a bathtub I would pull somebody's feet inside the sewer.
If I were a building I would throw out King Kong.
If I were sand I would bury myself.
If I were sand I would throw myself in bad boys' eyes.
If I were sand I would turn myself into a castle for bugs.
If I were a lizard I would go on dates with a cute rattlesnake.
If I were President I would give the poor people chocolate milk.
If I were President I would give people jobs mopping the floor.
If I were President I would free the people.
    —*First grade class*

If I were a principal I would:
give announcements
wash the dishes
relax in my chair and tell Phyllis to hold my calls
write good and bad notes to the mothers and fathers
    —*Second grade class*

If I were a poet I would:
eat, drink, and write love poems
write poems about dinosaurs, monsters, camels, and tapeworms
    —*Second grade group*

If I were grass I would:
get fallen on by a person who tripped
grow

get stepped on
get eaten by a cow
sit in the park
be raked away and die
eat the cow's insides after I was eaten by it
get mown off by mowers
fall down
be beautiful
go to sleep
turn into flowers
get eaten by a giraffe and get dizzy falling down his neck
get sprinkled
put a sign on me saying Please Keep Off
    —Kindergarten and first grade class

If I were peanut butter I would stick wall-to-wall in your mouth
If I were a black hole I would take in everything
If I were a kiss I would last long
If I were a boy I would go with me
If I were time I would take people back to their happy days
If I were sleep I would have dirty dreams
If I were love I would last eternally
If I were a number I'd go higher
    —Eighth grade group

If I were a poet I would:
tell the story I want to tell now
write poems about flowers and sandwiches
write poems about angels
just sing a song
do construction work
write my poems twice and xerox them
    —Kindergarten and first grade class

If I were a lizard I would:
leap around the leaves
squeak
do nothing
crawl in puppets
hide in the bedroom
slobber
    —Kindergarten and first grade class

•

To introduce dream poems, I talk about dreams with the class. Students love these discussions. I point out how varied our dreams are—sad, happy, mysterious, funny, sexy, silly, or terrifying. Some of us remember them, others don't—or don't try. When I remember mine I write them down in a dream journal. In *The Writing Workshop (Vol. 2)*, Alan Ziegler says, "Paying attention to my dreams tends to make subsequent dreams more interesting. Perhaps the unconscious does better when it has an audience." Also, spontaneously and quickly making up dreams and telling or writing them can be as dream-like as dreams themselves. Sometimes when students can't remember their dreams, I ask them to invent some.

One night I had a dream that I was Superman.
Another night I was God.
Last night I was the President.
Friday night I was myself.
　　　　　—Kurtis Wheatley, sixth grade

I dreamt that our apple tree had red, white, and blue apples on it.
I dreamt that the water in the water fountain was going in, not out.
I dreamt we got a new car but the tires were square.
I dreamt we had a couch but the couch was a big banana split.
I dreamt once that the earth was flat.
Once I dreamt in January the sun was out, the pool was frozen, some
　　　trees were bare and some were blooming.
Once I dreamt that a dog had a cat's tail, a mouse's nose, and a giraffe's
　　　neck.
Once I dreamt that I had a big red dog that I could ride on.
I dreamt that I had a giant notebook that I could climb into.
I dreamt that I was as tall as a giraffe.
　　　　　—Mary Beth Pala, Fifth grade

People

I dreamt I went to a land that had no people, just animals.
I dreamt the world I saw of animals, the land was beautiful and all the
　　　animals were free, NO LEASHES, NOTHING!! They were free
　　　at last!

Till I dreamt the next night something terrible. People—
People were being born and the dream broke right in half.
They leashed the poor animals and the broken dream was
destroyed and never to be dreamt again. That's why this
is so original.

PEOPLE!!
destroyers!!

—Wendy Travers, fifth grade

I dreamt that a big yellow dog was biting me and I pulled off his head
and it was my father!

I dreamt about me getting squashed under the stove.

I dreamt about when we lived on 71st Street, the lady next door
(Marie) gave me seven tiny, tiny puppies that fit in my hands but
they were all wet and dead.

I dreamt I had a lollipop but it started to taste like fish.

I dreamt that I was on a trampoline and went so high my head hit the
ceiling and I got stuck up there, then my mom got mad 'cause I
wouldn't come down and tried to pull my feet but my shoes came
off and mom fell down and got stuck in the floor and couldn't get
out.

I dreamt I ate cookies all day and they just kept going on in my stomach.

I dreamt a train was going to run over me and when I woke up my cat
was sitting on me.

I dreamt red guns were crying.

I dreamt I was getting married to Ronald McDonald and little Big Macs
were the bridesmaids.

I dreamt God took my hand but it came off in his hand.

I dreamt everybody was at my birthday and I had to sing Happy
Birthday but I only could burp.

I dreamt crayons melted in my pockets and all down my pants.

I dreamt my mom was giving me a spanking but it felt like feathers and
we were just laughing.

I dreamt a black cat was sitting on my chair laughing.

I dreamt I was driving a Cadillac chasing a robber and almost ran over
a skunk.

I dreamt I was walking up an orange spiral staircase.

I dreamt that everybody was going to get killed so when I ran out in
the street looking for my mom I saw everybody was having a block
party. When I told everybody there was going to be danger they
said, "Have a weenie!"

—Third, fourth, and fifth grade group

Koch's simple *I Used To/But Now* idea for a catalog poem about change is a favorite of children, especially in the lower grades. There are a number of nice surprises here.

I used to be a police dog but now I am a policeman
I used to be a married girl but now I am a farmer
I used to be a cloud in the sky but now I am a bluebird
I used to be a garbage can but now I am cookies
I used to be snow but now I am ice
I used to be a nose but now I am a sneeze
I used to be a newspaper but now I am a book
I used to be sunshine but now I am moonshine
I used to be a principal but now I am a prince
I used to be beautiful but now I am a girl
I used to be an apple but now I am a seed
I used to be a kitten but now I am a scratch
I used to be a little boat but now I am a cruise ship
I used to be a teacher but now I am a talking whale
I used to be Abraham Lincoln but now I am the Lincoln Tunnel
I used to be a good computer man but now I am a good typewriter man
I used to be a baby but now I am a writer
    —First grade class

I used to be Mother Nature but now I am chiffon
I used to be a lollipop but now I am a tongue.
I used to have freckles but now I have pimples.
I used to be a seed but now I am a pumpkin.
I used to be pink but now I am colorless.
I used to be a monkey but now I am Godzilla.
I used to put food in my hair but now I put it in my stomach.
I used to be babied but now I am yelled at.
    —Fifth grade group

I used to be a snowman but now I'm a puddle
I used to be a knight in armor but now I'm a pile of junk
I used to suck my thumb but now I bite my nails
I used to take a bath but now I take a shower
I used to drink grape juice but now I have come a long way to Hawaiian
    Punch
I used to climb the furniture but now I climb the trees
I used to be a devil but now I am an angel

I used to be the sun but now I am a speck of dust
I used to be in a crib but now I am in jail
I used to be bankrupt but now I am rich
I used to be teeth but now I am dentures
I used to be a cucumber but now I am a pickle
   —*Fourth grade group*

Chapter 9

How to Behave At a Fancy Party

This chapter discusses how to use rules, regulations, resolutions, and instructions to write list poems. Kids enjoy making and giving instructions, because it makes them feel powerful, like adults. Guidance or instructions often come in the form of a list. Recipes, for example, or dance steps. Biblical commandments. Game rules. How to build your own vacuum cleaner. How to paint the portrait of a bird.

To Do the Portrait of a Bird
to Elsa Henriquez

Paint first a cage
with an open door
then paint
something pretty
something simple
something beautiful
something useful
for the bird
then put the canvas against a tree
in a garden
in a wood
or in a forest
hide behind the tree
be quiet
don't move . . .
Sometimes the bird comes quickly
but it can also take many years
before deciding
Don't be discouraged
wait
wait even if it takes years
because the quickness or slowness of the bird's arrival

has nothing to do
with the success of the picture
When the bird arrives
if it arrives
observe the deepest silence
wait until the bird enters the cage
and when it has entered
quietly close the door with the brush
then
paint out all the bars one by one
being careful not to touch any of the bird's feathers
Then do the portrait of the tree
by picking its most beautiful branches
for the bird
paint also the green foliage and the freshness of the wind
the dust of the sun
and the sound of insects in the grass in the summer heat
and then wait for the bird to decide to sing
If the bird doesn't sing
it's a bad sign
a sign that the painting is bad
but if it sings it's a good sign
a sign that you can sign
So then you pluck very gently
one of the bird's feathers
and you write your name in a corner of the painting.
    —*Jacques Prévert, translated by Ron Padgett*

That was by a grown-up. These following examples by children, touching on morals, manners, and ethics, as well as practicalities, run the gamut from ironclad commandments to gentle suggestions.

How to Cook a Chicken

Unfreeze it with hot water
Let it settle
Clean it
Make sure it's dead
Scrape it
Season it with salt, pepper, flour
Put it in a pan with oil
Some onions

Green pepper
Garlic
String beans
Rice
Let it bake for 25–30 minutes
Serve with orange juice or milk
   —*Fourth grade group*

Recipe For Martin Luther King, Jr.

I. *Ingredients for Dream Man Cake*

7 gallons of love
10 cups of courage
10 cups of caring
1 quart of determination
500,000 tablespoons of heart
1 pinch of anger
40 tablespoons of peace
5 quarts of dreams
15 pinches of patience
20 pints of joy
40 dashes of honor
500 gallons of faith
10 quarts of hope
50 gallons of freedom
5 pints of responsibility
20 tablespoons of sadness
30 tablespoons of desegregation

II. *Directions*

Stir in love, mixed with courage, caring, and determination. Add heart by tablespoons with a pinch of anger. Peace and dreams are added slowly. Oh, don't forget the patience, joy, and honor added to complete faith and hope to give freedom to the growth of the cake. The responsibility gives a taste to the sadness and desegregation of the delicious cake. Then pop into the Holy Heaven Oven for one hour and presto!
   —*David Ramirez, fifth grade*

King Midas Touch

1 pound egg shells
2 pounds of mosquitoes (bones removed)
1 purple duck with polka dots
1 golden egg
A half of a frog
1 toenail of a dodo bird
3 feet of an ant (wash carefully)
1 eyeball of a cross-eyed bat
1 rose stem

Mix in the washing machine. Afterwards sprinkle on hands. Wait 3 hours, then touch everything in sight, except your friends. (Good way to get rid of enemies).

—Georgette Franzone and Janine Finlan, fourth grade

Chinese Ox Burger

Deep down in the ground you'll find many big oxes. Only one is Chinese—he'll have smaller eyes & a bigger head. Take a rag and treat him nice (Paul Bunyan method). . . . Say to the ox, "I'll give you anything you want in the whole wide universe!" The ox will follow you out of the hole wherever you go. Take him to the woods and give him a nice cup of tea. Then sneak up behind him, pour hot water and rice over his hide & shoot him with a machine gun until he's completely dead. Take off the skin, burn it, smoke it up with onions and Chinese spices (doodah, mugga, cunk, dit, kunga, & fronde). Boil in hot water, pour on cold water, spices, rices. Wait till it shrinks. (Play cards while waiting.) Serve in 9 portions.

—Crowder Brothers, second grade

How to Dance

Two feet dance. The left foot moves on the floor. The right foot taps on the floor. The record player plays green music. Then it stops. They stop dancing, and put another record on. Same thing. They eat milk and chocolate chips.

—Lisa Fox, first grade

The Book Dance

Take a book and put it on your head;
Take another book and tie it on your feet;
Jump around and roll your eyes.
    —Lenore Reich, first grade

The Fig (A Dance)

I see Ben in the house all day.
He do not go in the houses   (He dance like a fig)
doing the fig Hi He say by by   (He just roll his self)
Hi and by and by   (Over)
    —Ycarra Tabb, preschool

How to Behave at a Fancy Tea Party

Wear a black or brown suit or a pink or green dress.
Serve the cakes and cookies politely.
Eat slowly and quietly.
Swallow your food before you say anything.
Do not criticize your neighbor.
Make a compliment about your neighbor's shirt or blouse.
Talk about the weather, school, games, dogs, and clothes.
Say, "May I have the salt please?"
Smile and bow.
    —Ronald Jones and Keisha McBride, second grade

How to Keep Clean

Take a bath
Keep your clothes clean
Wash them
Wash your face
Brush your teeth
Wash your ears
Throw water in them
Behind your ears
Polish your shoes
Clean 'em with a rag
Splash water in your eyes
Wash out your eyes

Wipe off your nose with a face cloth
Wash your mustache with soap and water
Use wood fingercleaners for your fingers
Scrub your chest with Ivory Flakes
Stick your feet in boiling water
Give your elbows a mud bath
Mr. Brush will brush your knees
Stand by the radiator
Put heat through your body
Put a torch down your stomach
Take a white towel and dry yourself
Then take a bath!
    —Fourth grade class

How to Make Lots of Money

This is how to make lots of money.
First go to school and then go to high school
and then go to college and then get a job
and never get sick.
And never take a day off.
And go to work every day.
And try not to quit your job.
And don't let your boss fire you.
And go to work forever.
And never get a broken leg.
And never get hit by a car.
    —Taryn Dupree, third grade

Ways of Saying Good-bye

Good-bye
Bon jour
Peace
Adios
Good riddance
Hasta la vista
Bon voyage
Sai chin
So long
Leave
Farewell

Beat it
Scram
Va!
Get lost
Go run in traffic
It's been nice working with you
My heart breaks into small triangles as you go
Too bad you have to go
That's the way the block of ice crumbles
That's the way the blackboard cracks
When are you leaving?
          —*Fifth grade class*

People have a lot of problems and would like to do something about them. Improvement. There's always room for it. In school. At home. On the job. So, let's go America! And kids—do your part!

School As It Should Be
(Rules for Behavior and General Improvement)

If people fight I will make them fight in a boxing ring.
School should be fun.
No making out in the halls.
I will allow no smoking.
People should not cut class.
No hitting teachers.
I shall have a little arcade room.
For lunch, cheeseburgers every day.
If children keep fighting, they will go home for the rest of the week.
Have a drug alarm in case anybody brings drugs into the school.
A little candy store in the halls.
Talking back to elders, carrying weapons, instigating trouble will not
     be allowed.
I would have a lot of questions on lunchroom napkins and also PROBLEM
     OF THE DAY (if you answer correctly you win an adventure book).
Lunch period would be more exciting because instead of playing there
     would be exercise—gymnastics, climbing ropes, going through
     obstacle courses.
I would give fighting children a chance to explain themselves and make
     them apologize to each other.
We should have young teachers.
We could have a double dutch team.

We could have Bart Simpson shirts.
No throwing food.
No talking while the teacher is talking.
Do the right thing!
> —*Adrianne Davis, Jose Liriano, Joesian Danizard, Amanda Raysor,*
> *Serita Hall, Francine Laurel, sixth and seventh grades*

Seven Ways to Improve Boys

1) Kill them
2) Make them come alive and kill them again
3) Kill them again for fun
4) Punish them
5) Whip them
6) Put them in prison
7) Pull off their ears
> —*La Guire Wearing, Carlos Iglesia, Joanne Colon, Steven Rodriguez,*
> *and Cleveland Dan Thomas, second grade*

Ways to Improve My Life

study
read
pay attention
clean up better
have more understanding for people
leave New York
move to Chicago
become a journalist
be patient
don't talk back
stay in school
develop strong bones
keep my room clean
save money
don't marry ugly people
keep myself in check
no drugs
love one another
> —*Tina Valcarcel, Latrice Williams, Charlene Thurton, Jakanta Leggett,*
> *Tifereth Francis, and Anngelee White, sixth grade*

New Year's Resolutions (1988)

Fall in love
Visit the library once a week
Take music lessons
Study harder—read and write—concentrate—take notes—quiz
    yourself—be tested—keep a journal—team up with a friend—
    participate in more class activities
Listen
Learn
Keep better company—hang with people you trust
Help the elderly
Feed the needy
Give to the homeless
Work with charities
Respect others
Control your temper
Be more sympathetic, more understanding
Keep an open mind
Life is vulnerable, fragile, dear, precious—love it, cherish it
Overcome depression
Don't isolate yourself
Communicate with friends, family
Show you care about them
Cheer yourself up
Smile
Treat yourself to dinner at a French restaurant and a Broadway show
    (shouldn't cost more than $160, total, tops)
Take a vacation—Europe, Hawaii, Japan, Montreal, Paris, Jamaica,
Tahiti, France
Cruise the Pacific
Eat well—have as much seafood as you like
Keep clean
Pay attention
Love your elders, teachers, parents, yourself
    —Seventh grade group

The 15 Deadly Sins

It is a sin to eat with your hands
It is a sin to throw rocks at the church
It is a sin to rob a laundromat

It is a sin to rip out telephones
It is a sin to give a baby a poison needle
It is a sin to spill your juice
It is a sin to hit your landlord on the head with a vase
It is a sin to giggle with your mouth full
It is a sin to have a good time in school
It is a sin to eat jellyfish on Monday
It is a sin to pull down the wrong lever
It is a sin to burn alcohol
It is a sin to make fun of your generation
It is a sin to pour blood in the radio
It is a sin to make fun of the devil
    —*Third grade group*

Chapter 10

Menus, Haircuts, Fashion Notes, and Popular Dances

Menus, haircuts, fashions, and popular dances seem to go together because haircuts and dances are usually fads and relate to fashion, and because fancy restaurants are fashionable and food fads are always with us.

Kids know something about bad and strange food. I am alluding, of course, to the school lunch. So these invented menus should come as no surprise.

Disgusting Menu

SPECIAL TODAY—EAT ALL YOU CAN

squeezed eyeball in chalk juice   chocolate veins

frog on rye

string beans in gin   elephant guts

earlobe salad

eyelash pudding   buffalo milkshake

MIDNIGHT SNACK—Mint-flavored pig knuckles

hipbone jello   boiled stomach of dog

blueberry heart cake   lung chips

mice cream

hairballs in tears

poached dictionary

—Fifth grade group

Menu

Butterfly bones—$1.05

Bird guck—$1.10

Bird's liver marinated in sour cream with soy sauce & ketchup

with a side dish of milkweed—$2.45
Hippo skin with giraffe eyes—$1.50
TODAY'S SPECIAL
Pickled intestine & caterpillar sections
with either dinosaur juice or bee soup—8.78 francs
RETINA RUM
—Michael Olenick, fifth grade

Menu

3-legged Hungarian Dog Soup
muskrat tongue supreme
Brooklyn cobra
papreeeeeeeeeeeeeekah!!!!
torpedos
oiled roach rice
frozen Venetian carbon paper
Black Flag Cola
Dr. Jekyll's Blood Cookies
Vein noodle cookies
guppies in puke
belly button fluff
—Fifth grade group

Specials

Cream of steering wheel soup
Salade de Venus flytrap
Baked weeds in octopi oil
Ralph
Sauteed gorilla eyebrows in green snake sauce
—Sixth grade group

Some Sandwiches

a geology sandwich
a library paste sandwich on leather bread
a fox fur sandwich with red crayon dressing
a sandwich of the future! bread made out of ice! cheese made out of
    glass! butter of steel! rubber mayonnaise!
a polka-dotted yellowbelly sapsucker sandwich!
an oak tree sandwich

a little South American sandwich of anaconda and TNT
a coffin smeared with mustard and blood
a silver dollar sandwich with eagle sauce and George Washington's
    teeth sprinkled on it
a breath of fresh air sandwich
    —Sixth grade group

Baskin-Robbins

chocolate	black
vanilla	pizza
strawberry	graveyard dirt
butter pecan	blueberry
cocoa	adidas
banana	mice cream
peach	watermelon
dinosaur sherbet	green
cherry	dragon breath
pineapple	superfly
tea	neckbone
coconut	push-up
peanut butter	lime
soda	hang on
purple surprise	tiger
mint	afterburner
apple	d.j.
rainbow	safari
batman	pow
grapefruit	kung fu
cocktail	rose
mars	tyisha
charcoal	grape
oreo	orange

    —Fifth grade group

Hairstyles (for both sexes) have gotten weirder. Or maybe they always were weird—other than the standard "short back and sides" and an old-fashioned perm. These two haircut lists, like the Baskin-Robbins flavor list above, combine the real and made up.

Haircuts

butch
Afro
naps and peas
flathead
jeri curl
mohawk (Mr. T)
cameos
vees
finger waves
corn rows
french roll
Shirley Temple
pineapple waves
extensions
pinhead
mushroom
Congo
seesaw
punk rainbow
Don King fright wig
ponytail
pigtails
cocktails
bucket-cut
bowl-cut
chittlin' cut
Kojak
Buckwheat
chicken cutlet
Patty Labelle aircraft carrier
Tina Turner static control
Alfalfa state of shock
crewcut
box braids
Medusa
Watusi
grape soda
Eiffel Tower
conehead
uh-oh

coconut
bullethead
burr cut
egghead
   —*Eighth grade group*

One Thousand Haircuts

Batman, moose, Afro, fade, edge, spikes, Mohawk, pigtail, ponytail, curls, parasite, insect, aerobics, eagle, The W, The Z, levelheaded, dopey, flattop, draft, butterfly, horse, elephant, The Sparrow, salamander, Indian, flag, map, parrot, hippo, lion, robin, riddler, Joker, Mr. Freeze, penguin, King Tut, Lord Fog, musketeer, backstroke, tornado, balloon, leopard, tiger, Grumpy, mop, hip, sword, grizzly, lizard, newt, Simpson, ambulance, bathroom, lunch, monkey, raspberry, Toyota, crazy glue, globe, zodiac, mega, jackal, hawk, The Book, red scorpion, cobra, trapper, kingsnake, Medusa, stegosaurus, contra, alpha, fang, T, vampire, schoolbus, Muffy, idiot, worm, barbecue, half-moon, shave, smack jack, baseball, eyeballs, Pogo, Cupid, Jordan, I'm in Love Again, wheelcut, Who's Looking at Me?, street, roach, muppet, sunshine, turtle, Tweety, open your heart.
   —*Davon Valentine and Jelir Santiago, fourth grade*

Clothes consciousness begins early in life. Each grade level seems to have its own fashion standards, fads, and dos and don'ts. In the following poems though, kids were encouraged to go a bit wild and innovate. I'd love to see these outfits come traipsing down the runway.

Fashion Notes

A mask of purple toothpicks
Pink silk cockroach sandals
Wolf-hair sneakers
Pig ear & potato chip hat with cherry on top
Green brick pants
One-arm, two-belted disco-fever machine jacket
R-shaped shoes from Feetland
Cherry punch socks
Slow-water turtleneck
M & M coat of paint
Pushbutton interior raincoat

Plastic skunk-needle shirt
"Button-on" underwear
Jamaican Day Glo Boots
Clean Mean Teen Green Bean Jeans
Rectangular wool bathing suit
The Kitten's Mittens
Liver gloves
Long shorts
Chilly Willy copper & sea-blue tuxedo
Goat fur coat
Peacock feather waterproof pantyhose with trap door
Santa Claus alligator skin stockings
Sweaty-weather sweater
Wiggy boogy silver birthday peach monkey electric blue zoot suit
Kennedy cape
Anna Banana midi 2-split skirt
Rolling donut flap cap
Jellybelly jogging outfit
Get Down Wake Up & Boogie Till You Drop Dead dress
  —*Fourth grade group*

Fashion Show

Silk wildcat sweatband
Pink straw beret
Turquoise diamond earmuffs
Copper rimmed X-ray 3-D ghost glasses
Popcorn-shaped rubber nose-warmer
Taiwanese radio earrings
Nose ring to smell shapes
Live king cobra necklace
Boa constrictor tie
Dinosaur tooth scarf
Twinkling goldenrod Arizona asteroid shirt with purple popout
  pockets
Cement dancing blazer
Electric tension rock and roll sweater that does your homework
Overwear undercoat
Cowskin knickers over salt-and-pepper pantyhose
Garter snake belt
Glowing gum socks
Pumpernickel quarter loafers
  —*Second grade group*

The Castle Walk, the Lindy, the Mashed Potato, and the Electric Slide have come and gone. The following dance crazes came and went only in the minds of the authors.

The Banana Ballet Twist
The Pioneer Charleston
Wigglesworth
The Indian Flood & Combat
The Ugly
The Cross-eyed Centipede Waltz
Beachball Stomach Bounce
Gluefoot
Slide to Glory
The Ghost Drift
The Mummy Stumble
Paralyzed Jellyfish
The Chinese Windmill
Frank's Trap Door
Wiggle off the Edge of the Earth
Octopus on Fire
The Boston Jump
The Helium Pumpkin Roll & Display
The President's Dynamo Eyebrows
The First Impression Tango
The Wild Wire Wiggle & Wave
Crashing through the Night
Cookies and Champagne
Twin Towers Collapse
Rocket to Pathmark
Knockdown, Open Up, and Explode
Fishbone Rattle
Twirling Babies of the South
Teresa's Trampoline
The Nose
One Leg and Pray
Swinging Sandwiches
The Nap
The Foggy Trot
Walk around the Fat Lady
Line Up by Height
Utility Vehicle
Fast Forward

Take Off Your Glasses and Fly
The Bed-Stuy Bounce
Magic Moves
Spinning Skeletons
The Upsidedown Ski Jump
Spaghetti in Trouble
Dance of the Funky Professor
Galloping Cucaracha
The Discipline Waltz
Midgets on Stilts
    —Fourth to eighth grade groups

If you're feeling adventurous, have your students actually do the dances whose names they invent.

Chapter 11

Ingredients

Poets John Ashbery and Kenneth Koch once wrote some collaborative poems with special rules they made up. Each line had to contain certain "ingredients." For instance, in "Crone Rhapsody," every line has a flower, a tree, a fruit, a game, a famous lady, the word *bathtub,* and, at the very end, a piece of office furniture—all in the form of a sestina! The result is decidedly offbeat, childlike, and exhilarating:

Crone Rhapsody
(excerpt)

"Pin the tail on the donkey," gurgled Julia Ward Howe. A larch shaded
the bathtub. From the scabiosa on the desk
The maple gladioli watched Emily Post playing May I? in the
persimmon bathtub with the fan.
"Nasturtiums can be eaten like horseshoes," murmured the pumpkin,
"but on Hallowe'en when Cécile Chaminade's Rhapsody roars in
the beeches and a bathtub chair
Holds Nazimova, a lilac palm plays mumbledy-peg with an orange
bathtub filing cabinet,
And Queen Marie of Roumania remembers the Norway maple."
Pitching pennies from the canteloupe bathtub, I remembered the
poppy and the typewriter,
The mangrove and the larkspur bathtub. I saw a banana Carrie Nation
ducking for apples in the lamp.

Oak dominoes filled the bathtub with a jonquil. A crab-apple rolled
slowly toward the Edith Wharton lamp,
Crying, "Elm shuffleboard! Let the bathtub of apricots and periwinkles
give May Robson a desk!"
"Heavy, heavy hangs over thy head," chanted the black raspberry. A
zinnia dropped from the plane tree into a rotting bathtub. Dame
Myra Hess slumped over the typewriter
And wrote, "Dear Madame de Farge: A sycamore, an aster, and a
tangerine, while playing scrub in my bathtub, noticed a fan

Of yours. Do you remember the old cottonwood tree by the auction
     bridge? It's now a bathtub. The freesia is gone. And an apple placed
     Queen Victoria in the filing cabinet.
Forget me not, as Laura Hope Crewes once spelt out in anagrams while
     we were all eating honeydew melon. I write you this from the
     bathtub and from a willow chair."

A raspberry bathtub was playing leapfrog with Sarah Allgood in the
     heather. Junipers hemmed in the yellow Ukrainian chair.
In the apple tree Queen Mary of the Chrysanthemums shared a grape
     rook bathtub with her insect lamp.
The cranberry juice was playing water polo with the dwarf plum tree.
     Margaret Dumont approached the bathtub. A song came from
     within the wisteria-covered filing cabinet—
The gooseberries were playing golf! Louisa May Alcott lifted a water
     lily from the poison-oak bathtub: "Put this on the desk,
Mrs. August Belmont." In the poison sumac grove a spitting contest
     was in full swing. The bathtub peeled seven mangoes, and a
     petunia fan,
Known to the orchid prune as Dame May Whittie's bathtub, felt
     curvaceous playing house with a eucalyptus typewriter.
[. . .]

Seven ingredients in each line may be too many for children to
handle well, but you get the idea. Simplified schemes can be used,
such as using a color, an animal, and an action verb in each line:

Zoo Poem with Colors

The pink frog ate a carrot
Orange mice took my fingers
The red spider climbed up to the roof
The blue fish is playing ball
The gold hippopotamus took pictures of blackbirds
Brown ants took naps and dreamed of pink sheep
Red cobras boxed with gold lizards
Yellow horses shot french fries at silver worms
Green dinosaurs ran up and down the backs of pink mosquitoes
The brown dolphin swam all the way to Mexico
The purple monkey hopped to Key Food

A white bear slept like a baby
Some black mice bit my toes
A yellow seal made a mess under her desk
The green hippopotamus floats on her back
The orange turtle took a long walk in the woods
    —*Second grade class*

Taking the same scheme, some fifth graders added a foreign country. This greatly expanded the feeling of breadth in the poem. The ingredients themselves determine the nature of the poem to some extent.

Smashing Carrots in Mexico

The pink ladybug crawled over the Japanese dinner plate.
The red mouse ran across the Alaskan carpet.
A grape elephant jumped on the English cocoa can.
An orange turtle flew in the Colombian sky.
The yellow dinosaur ate the Mexican potato chips.
A red rooster soared across Russia in a jet.
The green giraffe ran after the timetable tree and ate all the leaves in
    Ecuador.
The pink monkey sat on a chair in Pennsylvania.
The white bunny ran through the farmer's farm and smashed all the
    carrots in Mexico.
The green turtle poked his face out of his shell and realized he was no
    longer in Peru.
The sneaky fish leaped over the school in Japan.
The yellow snake was laughing in the Russian closet.
The green tiger ate a Jewish Christmas tree.
The clock and the cat went cuckoo.
The brown cow ran to Canada to meet the plane.
The gorilla lives in a purple forest in China and spends his whole day
    sitting on a log.
The rat ran over the turquoise tracks.
The pink giraffe smashed the Peruvian coffee cup.
    —*Fifth grade group*

Speaking of foreign countries, some other fifth graders wrote excellent "travel" poems. The only required ingredient was the name of a country in each line, but the kids added lots of other interesting stuff.

Travel

In Italy I photographed the statue of Pope John Paul
The Queen of Spain autographed my teddy bear
Greek gods with the power of lions growled at our boat
Peaches in Israel were wilting in the sun
The lieutenant told us about the war in Vietnam
I had lunch with King Tut in the pyramids
Big Ben ticked and tocked all day long in London
Snakes zigzagged to the Indian flutes
The Russians were rushing to their jobs
Chinamen bowed low in their flowery cotton robes
Ecuador gave us mangoes and pineapples for breakfast
Steel drums bonged for us at a party in Trinidad
We skied down a mountain of Swiss cheese
The gauchos galloped across the pampas
Brazilians fed broccoli to their snakes and parrots
In Canada the ice evaporated on our suitcases
Boxing kangaroos carried the mail in their pouches
Hitler's German shepherd (Herman) bit our tour leader
Thai farmers were bending in the rice fields
In Iran poor people drilled for oil
We ate raw fish in the temples of Japan
Bongos boomed in the Cuban sugarcane
Bruce Lee leaped out of his buggy in Hong Kong
African ladies proudly steadily slowly smoothly trot with straw baskets
    of beans on their heads
    —Fifth grade class

The International Situation

Canada sneaks off to the jailhouse
Brazil puts peanut butter on her face
Russia makes a volcano of mayonnaise and baloney
Ireland snores and wakes up the dead
Ghana's writing its name in strawberry juice
Egypt is frying macaroni for dinner
South Africa makes red cheese under the table
USA is climbing up a ladder of boogers
Mexico grows a mustache of leather silk
Australia discovers the ladies' bathroom
Japan turns on a dim light

Mainland China is writing a letter to the zoo
England is swimming in a pool of dew
France looks out through windows baked in mustaches
Scotland crochets socks out of spider webs
Switzerland plants light bulbs in the garden
Chile is putting ice cubes in the snow
Italy is killing snakes making noise on the piano
Guam is making rat-proof boots
The Pacific Ocean conquers the world
and the countries turn into rock stew
    —Fifth grade group

The Song of the World

Costa Rica writes THE SONG OF THE WORLD on the black-board
Mexico fixes ham sandwiches for neighboring countries
Poland plays polo with a ping pong ball
Australia grins with her feet (by wiggling her toes)
Pakistan packs satin ears in a red rubber pack
Scotland drinks Scotch while riding a scooter to Nova Scotia
Japan jumps into a frying pan to sizzle for an hour
West Germany brushes her germs off on East Germany
Brazil put her baby on the windowsill
The Netherlands whips off his clothes and changes into The Superlands
Israel isn't really Israel—it's real estate
France dances fast with ants in her pants
Tanganyika dances the tango in the laundromat
Canada cans bananas for poor grandpas and grandmas
Panama makes plans for pancakes in pans
Puerto Rico cooks her rice in plain jelly
Russia brushes her hair with lots of pressure in the Gold Rush days
Iran away
Afghanistan knits afghans for Mozambique
Madagascar gives out cigars when he's mad at his guests
Chile freezes
Italy isn't an it—she slaps your face
It's Venezuela's birthday—Happy Birthday, Venezuela!
Haiti hates tea with sugar
Turkey bathes in gravy and sings THE SONG OF ASIA
Libya pours Libby's string bean juice on Women's Liberation
Austria plays with a rattle and goes goo-goo
Argentina gets tattoed by Chile

Guam chews gum
Yugoslavia stomps on Czechoslovakia
Czechoslovakia cries as he writes out a check to Medicaid
The United States meditates.
Come to beautiful Hungary if you want a full-course dinner!
   —*Fifth grade group*

Returning to the spirit of "Crone Rhapsody," we have an animal-color-bathtub poem and a series of famous-lady-plus-other-ingredients poems. Reading these mix-and-match structures is good brain-food for children. It satisfies their taste for gamesmanship while helping to develop their organizational skills.

Song of the Bathtub

A black donkey jumped screaming into the bathtub full of raisin juice!
A bluebird took a bath with my parakeet.
A white monkey played Nintendo in his bathtub.
An orange lion combed his hair in the bathtub.
A pink pit bull smelled yellow roses in my bathtub.
A white rabbit smoked a cigar in the bathtub.
I sat in a bathtub full of black water and a big green duck fell on my
   head!
A little silver cat danced the electric glide in my big bathtub.
The purple snake smashed the bathtub on the floor.
An orange bear came and ate the old bathtub.
Three gray horses jumped over the bathtub.
A dog named Blue sang and chewed gum in the bathtub.
A blackbird had a little bathtub on his head full of bird food.
A big tan pig sat in a tub full of mud.
A lady canary sat in a bathtub full of red hot blood.
Gray mice were killed by goldfish in my bathtub.
My bathtub is full of red rats.
Pink walls had a red tub with a unicorn in it.
My gold bulldog emptied the bathtub into the sink.
   —*Fifth to seventh grade group*

Famous Women

Aretha Franklin in a granny gown makes a sacrifice fly through the
   window of Woolworth's

Diahann Carroll jumped rope wearing a hot pants set with a midi vest
made out of wood tables while buying food for her kids at the
Puerto Rican store
Elizabeth Taylor, at Met Foods, was leaping triangular hurdles of
striped silk, wearing steel slacks
Barbara McNair, in a striped shift made out of Reynolds Wrap, threw
glass triangles at Jimmy Durante in Bruno's Hardware Store
Lucille Ball, riding on a vacuum cleaner in Bush and Smith's Drug-
store, took a set shot in a snow and heat wave into a puddleful of
basketballs
Mary McCloud Bethune, with an orange pantsuit on, put lipstick on
her watch to make time as red as something out of the lagoon
where they were building Macy's out of seaweed
  —*Fourth to seventh grade group*

Famous Ladies, Furniture, and Vegetables Ride Again!!!!!

White chairs danced around the Zsa Zsa Gabor cucumber!
The carrot of the ironing board exploded in the blue face of Betsy Ross!
Mary Todd cut her string beans with a yellow laser beam lamp!
A green bathroom scale squeezed tomato juice on the gloves of Nancy
Hanks!
Aida swallowed a small purple dresser stuffed with cabbage!
Rotten coconuts rolled over the Raquel Welch-red rug!
The Helen Keller end tables crushed the pale green radishes!
Corn sofas leaked on Snow White!
Mrs. Babe Ruth rubbed peas under the golden sink!
Mary Tyler Moore tossed salad onto a red bed!
Mixed vegetables ran screaming out of Mrs. Appleseed's blue piano!
Jane Addams jumped up and down on a white hot potato stove!
  —*Fourth to seventh grade group*

Famous Ladies Revisited

Gray filing cabinets stole second holding a papaya rickey once owned
by Joan Crawford
Marian Anderson prepared for a set shot over the blue typewriter by
swallowing pickle juice
Lavender Pepsi was poured into the President's swivel chair by Martha
Washington in the end zone: touchdown!
  —*Fourth to seventh grade group*

Chapter 12

Rhymed Couplets
(List Poems Inspired by Walt Whitman and Thanksgiving)

Reading Walt Whitman's poem "I Hear America Singing" made me think that it would make a good starting point for a writing assignment for some third graders I'd been working with.

I Hear American Singing

I hear America singing, the varied carols I hear,
Those of mechanics, each one singing his as it should be blithe and
    strong,
The carpenter singing his as he measures his plank or beam,
The mason singing his as he makes ready for work, or leaves off work,
The boatman singing what belongs to him in his boat, the deckhand
    singing on the steamboat deck,
The shoemaker singing as he sits on his bench, the hatter singing as he
    stands,
The wood-cutter's song, the ploughboy's on his way in the morning,
    or at noon intermission or at sundown,
The delicious singing of the mother, or of the young wife at work, or
    of the girl sewing or washing,
Each singing what belongs to him or her and to none else,
The day what belongs to the day—at night the party of young fellows,
    robust, friendly,
Singing with open mouths their strong melodious songs.

Together we would create a catalog of all kinds of people singing their "varied carols." Maybe we'd have animals and inanimate things singing, too. I suggested that we start the poem with "I hear American singing." Then we'd list who or what was singing— teacher, policeman, nurse, toaster oven—and what was being sung.

But the kids wanted to make rhymes. They insisted that "I hear the bells ringing" be the next line. I gave in and the work became a list poem in rhymed couplets. The first line of each couplet followed a format: "I hear (something) (making some sound)," e.g., "I hear the windows slamming." Then we'd get a rhyme (another participle) for the next line: "jamming," for example. Who or what was doing the jamming? "Jelly." In other words, in the second line of each couplet, we worked backwards, getting the rhyme first and then the start of the line. This jumping around in the composition keeps the ideas and images fresh, as opposed to trying to write all the lines "straight out." Most of the couplets are about hearing, but some are about other senses. I suggested that all the poems begin and end with Whitman's title to give a sense of unity and closure.

I think these collaborations reflect Whitman's music and multifariousness even though I read the Whitman example only to the older (sixth grade) students. And their being collaborations by fifteen or more children makes them as diverse and populated as Whitman's poem.

I Hear America Singing

I hear America singing
I hear the bells ringing
I hear the glasses clinking
I hear the teachers drinking
I hear the drivers driving
I hear the nurses arriving
I hear water dripping
I hear my pants ripping
I hear the eggs frying
I hear the liars lying
I hear the mice squeaking
I hear the sneakers sneaking
I hear the ghosts booing
I hear the bunnies chewing
I hear the saw sawing
I hear the grandmas sewing
I hear the clock ticking
I hear feet kicking
I hear the pencils writing
I hear mosquitoes biting
I hear the money jingling
I hear the spines tingling
I hear birds tweeting

I hear fat guys eating
I hear the chairs scraping
I hear prisoners escaping
I hear dreamers dreaming
I hear the babies screaming
I hear the tongues clicking
I hear the glue sticking
I hear Santa's stomach jiggling
I hear the girls giggling
I hear the lions roaring
I hear the grandpas snoring
I hear the poodles snapping
I hear the hands clapping
I hear the vines clinging
I hear America singing
    —First grade class

I Hear America Singing

I hear America singing
I hear the bells ringing
I hear the tiger stalking
I hear the parrot talking
I hear the orange squeezing
I hear the Arctic freezing
I hear the dogs barking
I hear the Chevrolets parking
I hear the babies crying
I hear the football flying
I hear the birds screeching
I feel the arms reaching
I hear the cat scratching
I hear the eggs hatching
I see the yuppies drinking
I hear the divers sinking
I hear the dolls dancing
I feel the eyes glancing
I hear the South Pacific splashing
I feel the potatoes mashing
I hear the blood flowing
I see the needles sewing
I hear the wind blowing

I hear the mowers mowing
I see the snow snowing
And the professors knowing
I hear the swings swinging
I hear America singing.
    —*Kindergarten and first grade group*

I Hear America Singing

I hear America singing
I hear the bells ringing
I hear rattlesnakes rattle
I hear the armies battle
I hear the people talking
I hear the children walking
I hear the birds flying
I hear babies crying
I hear rabbits jumping
I hear hearts pumping
I hear dancers stomping
I hear donuts dunking
I hear birds tweeting
I hear belts beating
I hear pages turning
I hear bushes burning
I hear throats coughing
I hear hyenas laughing
I hear pencils tapping
I hear flags flapping
I hear squirrels squeaking
I hear faucets leaking
I hear dogs barking
I hear cars parking
I hear beavers chopping
I hear mommies shopping
I hear rain falling
I hear grandmas calling
I hear pinballs rolling
I hear daddies bowling
I hear papers folding
I hear teachers scolding
I hear kangaroos bouncing

I hear eagles pouncing
I hear ants hustling
I hear cowboys rustling
I hear wolves howling
I hear bears growling
I hear the stars twinkling
I hear the cakes sprinkling
I hear cigarettes smoking
I hear the clowns joking
I hear windows slamming
I hear jelly jamming
I hear grown-ups arguing
I hear chefs barbequeing
I hear the trumpets swinging
I hear America singing
    —*Third grade group*

I Hear America Singing

I hear America singing
I hear the doorbells ringing
I smell the turkeys cooking
I see big brown eyes looking
I hear the fingers picking
I feel the dobermans licking
I hear the grandmas knitting
I see the kiddies kidding
I hear the Swatches ticking
I watch Darryl Strawberry hitting
I see the green eyes blinking
And blue eyes winking
I feel my old brain thinking
I see the *Titanic* sinking
I feel my stomach aching
Because I ate too much of my mother's baking
The sunburned skin is peeling
My father is fixing a hole in the ceiling
I see the customers eating
I see the noses bleeding
The fishermen are fishing
I hear the cat's tail swishing
I feel the fingernails scratching
I see the chickens hatching

149

And soldiers are attacking
I see the actors acting
I hear Uncle Louie snoring
The bulls are goring
Mrs. Conroy is teaching
One student is cheating
I see the dreamers dreaming
I hear my neighbor screaming
I see the moonlight beaming
Christmas bulbs are gleaming
I hear the lungs breathing
And babies are teething
I feel the bees stinging
I hear America singing
      —*Sixth grade group*

Another theme for a rhymed couplet came up one year around Thanksgiving. In a fourth grade class we were trying to work up a list poem of things the kids were thankful for. The results were predictable and flat. I can't remember how, but we kind of spilled over into speculating what Superman would be thankful for: "his cape." Then, one rhyme-happy kid said something silly using a cape/grape rhyme. We wound up with "Superman is thankful for his cape / Wine is thankful for a grape."

That started an avalanche of rhymed couplets. As in the Whitman couplets, we began by asking who or what was thankful for what? Then we'd get our rhyme and work in reverse. The kids loved the shifting, gamelike activity.

Thanksgiving

The pencils are thankful for their points
Knuckles are thankful for their joints
The sky is thankful for its birds
Letters are thankful for their words
Buttons are thankful for their coat
Tin cans are thankful for their goat
Typewriters are thankful for their keys
Honey is thankful for the bees
Hair is thankful for a head
Snow is thankful for a sled

A watch is thankful for its time
A poet is thankful for rhyme
Oxygen is thankful for breath
Worms are thankful for death
Earrings are thankful for ears
Ghosts are thankful for fears
Surgery is thankful for stitches
Scratches are thankful for itches
A brain is thankful for thinking
A fat man is thankful for shrinking
Elves are thankful for toys
Girls are thankful for boys
A bathing suit is thankful for a body
Bruce Lee is thankful for karate
A waffle is thankful for syrup
Make-up is thankful for a mirror
Fingernails are thankful for polish
A brain is thankful for knowledge
A microscope is thankful for a bug
Arms are thankful for a hug
A baby is thankful for Pampers
A tent is thankful for campers
A frank is thankful for mustard
A pie is thankful for custard
    —*Second grade group*

Poem of Thanksgiving

Pencils are thankful for their points
Bones are thankful for their joints
Waves are thankful for their water
Mother is thankful for her daughter
Guns are thankful for their bangs
Cobras are thankful for their fangs
Sweaters are thankful for their wool
Swimmers are thankful for the pool
Alligators are thankful for their bumps
Mashed potatoes are thankful for their lumps
A globe is thankful for its spin
Lips are thankful for a grin
A jacket is thankful for a zipper
Cinderella's thankful for her slipper

Readers are thankful for magazines
Weightwatchers thankful for Lean Cuisine
Acrobats thankful for a trampoline
Millionaires thankful for their limousine
Rappers are thankful for their raps
Bottles are thankful for their caps
Joggers are thankful for their laps
Dancers are thankful for their taps
Flies are thankful for the garbage
Landlord is thankful for the mortgage
Ghosts are thankful for their sheets
Cavities are thankful for some sweets
  —Third grade class

Grateful Words

The dog is thankful for his bone
The sculptor is thankful for his stone
The snake is thankful for its skin
The shark is thankful for its fin
The mustache is thankful for its lip
The jump rope is thankful for its skip
Airplanes are thankful for the air
Heads are thankful for some hair
Pencils are thankful for their points
Knuckles are thankful for their joints
A copycat is thankful for his neighbor
A baby is thankful for its mother's labor
A worm is thankful for dirt
A water pistol is thankful for a squirt
Arms are thankful for a hug
A frog is thankful for a bug
A flag is thankful for its pole
Rock is thankful for roll
A chicken's thankful for its wings
A park is thankful for its swings
Electricity is thankful for light
Manners are thankful for "polite"
The dinosaurs are thankful for their museum
Dr. Martin Luther King, Jr., is thankful for his dream
A teacher is thankful for her brain
The tracks are thankful for a train

A studio is thankful for its art
Love is thankful for a heart
　　—*Third to fifth grade group*

As a warm-up, you might want to read the first lines of some of these couplets to your students and have them supply new second lines.

Chapter 13

Grab Bag

There are many other possibilities for catalog poems. Here they are in all their messy glory, some of them beautiful or strange or both, all of them useful.

Similes

People—children especially—enjoy making comparisons. In a poem, similes can be an entertaining digression from the central idea: they can expand an image or scene, providing depth, suspense, decoration, or enhancement of beauty. Below are catalogs of similes on display for their own sake. These vary somewhat in aptness but they are often surprising and usually free from cliché.

Similes

The boy ran as fast as a speeding Lamborghini.
My brain is as small as a particle of a peanut.
The soldiers marched in like robot elephants.
His hands are as big as desks.
The old lady screamed like squeaking chalk.
He thinks as slow as seaweed in the ocean.
The dinosaur eats palm trees like a lawn mower on a golf course.
The burning space shuttle crashed like the stock market.
    —*Fifth grade group*

School is as dull as the Presidential debates.
You look like your nose was hit by lightning.
I am as skinny as half a toothpick.
The kids played the piano as good as Beethoven.
The earth is like a green blanket with holes.
Your legs are as thin as silk thread.
The line of traffic is like my zipper.
The lake is as dirty as my dad's socks.

Our phone bill is as high as the sky (it's my fault).
The volcano is like a mountain with hiccups.
The lion roared like an old trombone.
Snowflakes are like little icy mirrors.
Chalk is like a snail leaving a trail behind.
The clouds are like floating fountains.
The wind blows like a broken whistle.
Grass to an ant is like a dark forest.
Schoolbooks are like handcuffs in a prison.
A mobile is like a comet of objects.
Grumpy people are as sour as a lemon in a pickle.
　　—*Fifth grade group*

Now let's take a look at similes grouped around a single idea or image. It's curious to see them lined up like starlings on a clothesline.

A Poet

A poem is like a wheel
A poet is like a fish out of water
A poem could be anything
A poet can think of everything
A poet's power is as great as thunder
A poet leaves everyone in amazement and wonder
A poet is as mysterious as fog
He wanders in a cloud of thought
A poet leaves his image very blurred
A poet is like the high school band
A poet is better than creative writing
A poet is like the John Newbery Medal
A poet is like you and me only better
He has so many things going on in his head it's like a freeway
He makes Superman look like a jerk
A poet is like a wildflower blooming
A poet is like a wild animal
A poet is like a bandleader
A poet is like a popcorn machine
A poet is like a lighthouse shining on water, finding a way for others
A poet is not dumb
A poet is like a herd of buffalo
A poet is like the wind hitting against an old windmill
Sometimes a poet acts like a bird

155

A poem rings like a doorbell
A poet is a special person saying beautiful things, like a messenger of
    God
A poet is a hard worker
A poet never sleeps
A poet works all night
A poet recites in the shower
A poet is noisy
A poet is funny
A poet has holes in his head
A poet is heavenly
A poet has patience
A poet is beautiful
A poet is like a clock, every second ticking with new ideas
A poet is like a window opening up into different dimensions
A poet is like a fence stretching high for new thoughts
A poet is like a strawberry sundae with the world as a cherry
A poet is like an ape holding a banana
A poem is like fresh falling snow
A poem is like clouds never separating
A poem is like a newborn baby
A poem is a rocket going into space
A poem is like a rainbow
A poet is like a block of flowers
    —*Fifth grade group*

Openings

Poet Dick Gallup invented the openings poem for use in the
classroom. It's like a word association game: one thing instantly
reminds you of—and comes out of—another. I recommend quick,
spontaneous composition. That way, the kids may surprise themselves.
They think they know where their minds are leading them, but there
are plenty of slippery twists in store. As it proceeds, the poem picks
up an insistent, overheated rhythm, like a chant. Kids love hearing
them read aloud. The excitement is contagious.

The Discovery of Air

I opened the door and out came a lion
I opened the lion and out came a mouse

I opened the mouse and out came cheese
I opened the cheese and out came a butterfly
I opened the butterfly and out came butter
I opened the butter and out came a bee
I opened the bee and out came honey
I opened the honey and out came sugar
I opened the sugar and out came salt
I opened the salt and out came pepper
I opened the pepper and out came a sneeze
I opened the sneeze and out came a cloud
I opened the cloud and out came rain
I opened the rain and out came a rainbow
I opened the rainbow and out came gold
I opened the gold and out came silver
I opened the silver and out came money
I opened the money and out came change
I opened the change and out came a lollipop
I opened the lollipop and out came a stick
I opened the stick and out came wood
I opened the wood and out came fire
I opened the fire and out came water
I opened the water and out came fish
I opened the fish and out came bones
I opened the bones and out came a skeleton
I opened the skeleton and out came a spirit
I opened the spirit and out came The Devil
I opened the Devil and out came flames
I opened the flames and out came smoke
I opened the smoke and out came air
    —Fifth grade class

I opened the week and days came out
I opened the days and time came out
I opened time and numbers came out
I opened the numbers and letters came out
I opened the letters and rice came out
I opened the rice and Uncle Ben came out
I opened Uncle Ben and colors came out
I opened the colors and a rainbow came out
I opened the rainbow and the sun came out
I opened the sun and fire came out
I opened the fire and the fire department and water came out

I opened the water and pollution came out
I opened pollution and the universe came out
I opened the universe and planets came out
I opened the planets and the end came out
   —Linda Plofsky, sixth grade

I opened the door and out came a bear
I opened the bear and out came an octopus
I opened the octopus and out came a hat
I opened the hat and out came a man
I opened the man and out came the world
I opened the world and out came a squid
I opened the squid and out came ink
I opened the ink and out came a pen
I opened the pen and out came a pig
I opened the pig and out came bacon
I opened the bacon and out came fat
I opened the fat and out came skinny
I opened skinny and out came blood
I opened the blood and out came paper
I opened the paper and out came origami
I opened origami and out came blood vessels
I opened the blood vessels and out came string
I opened the string and out came a skeleton
I opened the skeleton and out came a shirt
I opened the shirt and out came pants
I opened the pants and out came teeth
   —Kindergarten and first grade group

In these three examples, notice that what comes out in one line gets opened in the following line. Such tight sequencing isn't necessary. Each line could begin a whole new subject.

Colors

Using colors profusely in poetry works especially well with younger students, who are excited by the brightness of primary colors. You can organize a list poem around one color or a rainbow.

Red

Red is for the lips on your face
Red is blood
Red is thick
Red is when I get sunburnt
Red is the color of my tie
Red is electric
Red is an arrow
Red is a shoe
Red is a termite under my shoe
Red is a whale kissing a goldfish
Red is rocky
Red is an octopus kissing me
Red is sick
Red is a big shot
Red is an apple
Red is a devil
Red is a Batman and Robin
      —*Seth Charnes, third grade*

Brown

Brown is tigers watching television
Brown is a bag
Brown is a Brownies outfit
Brown makes me feel kind of happy
Brown is a table and a chair
Brown is the wardrobe
Brown is two lions making a cake
Brown is okay and is helpful
      —*Maureen, third grade*

Yellow

Yellow is springy
Yellow is bright and golden
Yellow makes me feel cool and I feel like I'm under the sprinkler
And blond hair is yellow to me
Yellow tastes yummy
It makes flowers beautiful
Yellow is last but not least
      —*Grace Ann, third grade*

Yellow

A bee buzzes in the shining buttercups
As the sun glows on the Chinese students
Who are biting their pencils
Because they're going bananas
They've been out in the sun too long
The sunlight gently touches
The giraffe's neck
As it stretches over the fence to see
The blond lion tearing into a pineapple
   —Fifth grade group

Red

A newspaper is red all over
With photographs of Mars on fire
Fire engines fly to brick buildings
And the rescue of red-faced Martians
Who hold their breath in the blood-filled smoke
Back on earth, apples and cherries are picked
By hungry Russians and red Indians
With rosy cheeks, noses, and lips
Angry robins attack the roses
And drop rubies among the strawberries
   —Fifth grade group

Hotel Rainbow

A blue river rushes to the green ocean
Goldfish wiggle through beige-purple seaweed
Gray ships float to yellow-green Hawaii
Banana-colored hula skirts shake like strawberry milkshakes
Green palm leaves sway in the white breeze
In the red and gold hotel a navy blue bellboy carries the silver breakfast
    tray of orange tacos to the sleepy man in polka-dot pajamas
The red-orange sun rises in the morning, shining on the tan sand
Pink and purple parakeets splash in the marble green birdbath
A white letter is delivered to the sleepy man.
It's from Grandma. She says
Come back to the beautiful Bronx
Where the black smoke is flooding the gray sky!
   —Fifth grade group

Letters

The alphabet poem is about as basic as you can get, but no "A is for apple" for these kids. I encouraged them to go for the unusual. Their alphabets became pretty komplicated.

A is for AQUA
B is for BONUS
C is for CAPS
D is for DECIDE
E is for EXCITED
F is for FEDERAL
G is for GORILLA
H is for HECTOR
I is for INVESTIGATION
J is for JUNIOR
K is for KOMPLICATED
L is for LIGHT
M is for MAMMOTH
N is for NATIONAL
O is for OVAL
P is for PAIN
Q is for QUAKER
R is for RAZOR
S is for SYMBOL
T is for THAT
U is for UNITED
V is for VICTORY
W is for WONDER
X is for X RAY
Y is for YO-YO
Z is for ZONE
      —Third grade group

A is for armored tank
B is for bagel
C is for Cary Grant
D is for dislodge
F is for factory
G is for garbage man
H is for heavy

I is for impossible
J is for a jar of jelly
K is for Kentucky
L is for launching pad
M is for monstrosity
N is for neglected
O is for Oreo cookie
P is for Panasonic
Q is for quintuplets
R is for ruined
S is for squirt
T is for torture
U is for unicycle
V is for Vitalis
W is for wonderful wagon
X is for Xenia, Ohio
Y is for yodel
Z is for zinnia
　　　—*Fifth grade group*

Definitions

I was in a perverse mood one day, and asked a group of fifth graders to define words they probably wouldn't know (though some kids will surprise you). Though these "definitions" read more like imaginative lists than list poems, they delighted me, giving me an entirely new way to look at certain words—useful for any writer, including the students.

Fifth Grade Dictionary

spontaneous—exciting; to respond too much
domestic—train; to be romantic
misgiving—don't give; not to be given to that person
calamity—weight on something; pertaining to a calameter
herbal—person's name
pituitary—a kind of cemetery
Zuñi—a vegetable
corrugated—punishment
gracious—lively; thankful

panache—place on "All My Children"
obese—stop; to be jealous
trinket—noise made by water faucet
harpie—stringed instrument
cartouche—French for car; furniture
pinwheel—wheel with a pin in it
respite—Sprite mixed up with an extra "e"
trite—a flea
filigree—pertaining to temperature
blasé—French for blouse
    —*Fifth grade group*

Syzygy: a pair of surgical scissors
cairn: a piece of canned corn
mantissa: a beautiful dress
vacillation: Your arm is clean.
zephyr: a beautiful musical instrument that yodels
    —*Jonathan Rosenstein, fifth grade*

Quiz

The idea of a more elaborate quiz came from the definitions work (above). I usually try to make the questions either mysterious or direct and disarming. The kids respond in kind. The combinations result in some truly Rabelaisian lists, which I have put together from various kids' responses.

What Happens to You When You Are Psychoanalyzed?

You get very stupid
you become drunk
I become crazy every night
you do not know what you are talking about
I'll kill someone
to be on drugs
the teacher goes away
you talk or you die!!!
you get confused
you become a doctor
you get tortured by the Nazis

you fall off a couch
you pay $110
you lie down and talk to an old guy with a beard and glasses
I get bored
don't ask
I throw up
you get VD
you get to eat good things
you become a midget monster
you start crowing
you say KILL!
you shrink

What Did Your Face Look like Before You Were Born?

covered with candy and blood
I remember
Rudolph Valentino
it looked swollen and disfigured
flat like a pancake, sticky with maple syrup
a nonformed ball of flesh
a squashed tomato mixed with scrambled eggs
it didn't
Madagascar
Elizabeth Taylor
Julius Caesar
no hair
beautiful
Rock Hudson
crunkled
a baby face
paper
a prune
transparent
a ghost
like an angel
grasshopper
I couldn't see
probably very good looking

How Did the Egyptians Shine Their Shoes?

with their toes
with spit and sand
with cow's milk
they tried but they couldn't bend down
with their hair
they went to the barber and got a shine
sandpiper
with shoe polish
with their nose which they brushed with Crest
with hieroglyphics
with a shoe cleaning kit
they didn't wear shoes!
they polished their feet
with a lot of problems
in the Nile
with papyrus
with their tongues
with oil and a rag
in the sun
with their mittens

What Happens on the Other Side of the Mirror?

It's inside my sister's closet
no pollution
I'm the king
you're dead
you walk into the classroom on the other side and you learn everything
you see huge plants and a fairy queen made of flowers and you marry
    her and . . .
you fall off the Empire State Building and land on the Statue of Liberty
I went back
you've outnumbered yourself
I see a giant tube of Pepsodent
people will look at you
you meet Alice in Wonderland
everything is upsidedown and backwards
my reflection will come up to me and lead me to my quarters
you get to see a lot of yourself

I'll be eaten by an egghead
you go crazy
you see white rabbits
I'd see Henry Aldrich
it's Arizona
silvery paint chips will coat me
you get stuck in the wall
you see a miracle
you can see your ghost

What Is the Answer?

Huh?
What was the question?
Batman
dog
live
nothing
what
tree
book
The Daily Double
yes
1 or 5
the basketball is green
maybe
garlic & a sneeze
Pepi Alfonzo & Waneko Babino
NO!
14,000 were killed by crucifixion
don't be so smart!
Bolsheviks
a wart
no reply

What Is the Shortest Distance between Salt & Pepper?

when you put them close together
water
they don't taste so good

a-choo!
1 pizza
2 miles
sugar
1 millionth of a millimeter
the length of cinnamon
paprika
a molecule
who knows?
98.83 inches
garlic
vinegar
a potato
Irving
sugar drops
a close shave
ah?
Utah
a shake
a steak in rice and roll him in duck sauce
bring him to a Chinese laundry
Say "Ah, so!"
bow low
  —Sixth grade group

David Shapiro's "I Haven't" reads like an oral quiz in a dream:

I Haven't

Do you have a lion in your house?
Do you have a serpent in your house?
No fortunately I do not have a lion in my house.
Do you have a woman leaning slightly past the spirals in your house?
No I do not have the edge of her dress in my house.
Do you have a lion in your house?

No I do not have the outline of her body in my house.
Do you have a trouvaille in your house?
No fortunately I do not have a lion in my house.

Do you have the goddess Hygeia headless as a house?
No I do not have her right hand casting a shadow on my house.
Do you have a lion in your house?

No I do not have her light peplos folds full of life in my house.
Do you have "truth is the consequences" in your house?
No fortunately I do not have a lion in my house.

What do you have in your high heavy house?
Do you have a rendering of her brilliant pitiless hair falling on your
    house?
Do you have a lion in your house?
No fortunately I do not have a lion in my house.

Things I Don't Understand

Kids wonder about certain big and little things that seem mysterious, illogical, or somehow wrong. They don't always ask about them or get the chance to express their puzzlement. Here are some lists of what they don't "get."

I Don't Know About

banks
secretaries
principals
mayors
presidents
god
chinese people
horseshoes
    —*Doreen Reich, third grade*

Things I Don't Know (About)

horse's teeth
shorthand
secretary of state

quantum series
access road
vacuum tube
gravity flow water system
what a cooper does
ouija boards
     —Laura Olenick, fifth grade

Things I Don't Know About

gas
airplane
homes
tapes
art
factory
red, black badges
iron
winter solstice
begonias
tree shirt
rodent hair
vampire
tonsilectomy
     —Glen Ryan, fourth grade

Things I Don't Understand

Algebra, points of view, history, guns, autobiography, biography,
typewriters, technology, xylophones, organs, harmonicas, cashier,
cameras, computers, violins, electricity, football, cars, decimals.
    —Edward Rivera, fourth grade

Things I Don't Understand

One thing I don't understand is why my mother tells me to always wear
    the uniform.
But why do I always have to wear my uniform?
I still look the same with regular clothes.

Another thing I don't understand is why my mother doesn't let me
  wear hairspray.
But why can't I wear hairspray because even though I do or not do,
  my hair is always a mess.
Another thing I don't understand is BOYS. Such show-offs. It makes
  them look stupid.
Another thing I don't understand is math.
My teacher says math is your life.
But if math is my life why wasn't I born with math?
Another thing I don't understand is attitude.
People act all cool but inside they're wimps.
  —*Wanda Morales, fifth grade*

I'm not too sure about tree shirt and rodent hair, myself, or
gravity flow water system, either.

Lineups

Poet Charles North's idea for a list poem will charm kids and
teachers who are baseball fans, and who understand the subtleties of
batting orders and fielding positions. Almost any category can inspire
a lineup: Presidents, condiments, furniture, insects, you name it.
(Nonfans may exit the stadium and skip over to the next item.)

Vivaldi 3b
Chopin 2b
Mozart cf
Beethoven c
Wagner 1b
Brahms lf
Debussy ss
Handel rf
Bach p

Legs ss
Hips rf
Breasts 1b
Genitals lf
Buttocks c

Stomach cf
Feet 2b
Arms 3b
Head p

Orange ss
Blue lf
Green 3b
Purple cf
Red lb
Tan c
Brown rf
Pink 2b
Yellow p

For Girls Only

Anne Waldman's long chant-poem "Fast Speaking Woman" is like a hypnotic magic spell, with marvelous dynamic rhythms.

Fast Speaking Woman
(excerpt)

[. . .]
I'm the night woman
I'm the black night woman
I'm the night without a moon
I'm the angel woman
I'm the white devil woman
I'm the green skin woman
I'm the green goddess woman
I'm the woman with wings
I'm the woman with sprouts
I'm the woman with leaves
I'm the branch woman
I'm the masked woman
I'm the deep-trance woman

I'm the meat woman
I'm the red meat woman

I'm the fish woman
I'm the blue fish woman
I'm the woman with scales
I'm the woman with fins
I'm the crawling woman
I'm the swimming woman
I'm the sun fish woman
I'm the silver fish woman

        water that cleans
        flowers that clean as I go

I'm the moss woman
I'm the velvet moss woman
I'm the woman with vines
I'm the woman with thorns
I'm the needle woman
I'm the pine needle woman
I'm the science woman
I'm the mistaken woman
I'm the inexorable woman
I'm the explorer woman

I read an excerpt to a group of eighth grade girls and, almost at once, they created their own version about pride and the power of women.

Sunrise Woman

for Anne Waldman

I'm a daydreaming woman
I'm a back-to-nature woman
I'm a springtime woman
I'm a free-spirited woman
I'm a sunset woman
I'm a sunrise woman
I'm a sunny day woman
I'm a moonshine woman
I'm a butterfly woman
I'm a bird-watching woman
I'm a rainbow woman
I'm a man-hunting woman
I'm a nice young woman with everything

I'm a woman who is every man's dream
I'm a woman who's *really* a woman!
I'm a sexy black woman in a black negligee
I'm a together mama
I'm a poetry woman
I'm a woman who sings real dark
I'm a woman down the street
I'm a woman who flies in the night
I'm a red lady
I'm a girl with a cobra in her hair
I'm a girl with a l-o-n-g animal
I'm a crazy girl with a falcon
I'm a bear woman
I'm a slow-walking lady
I'm a big tall window woman
I'm a sad and loving woman
I'm a freaky little woman
I'm a short fat little woman
I'm a long-nailed monkey woman
I'm a weird window woman
I'm a purple woman
I'm a creepy spider woman
I'm a sleepy old lady
I'm an octopus woman
I'm a little TV girl
I'm an underarm girl
I'm a vindow viper girl
I'm a schveeper girl
I'm the justified woman who loves to understand
I'm a life woman
> —*Patty Lanza, Elizabeth Levenson, Carol Ann Mooney, Alice Pace, Lori Thomas, Kim Thompson, and Sonya Williams, eighth grade*

I, He, and She

As in Anne Waldman's poem above, the use of personal pronouns to begin each line of a poem is a simple and effective technique in catalog verse. The pronoun—especially *he* or *she*—takes on a mysterious, somewhat hieratic quality.

Ballade
(excerpt)

I know flies in milk
I know the man by his clothes
I know fair weather from foul
I know the apple by the tree
I know the tree when I see the sap
I know when all is one
I know who labors and who loafs
I know everything but myself.

I know the coat by the collar
I know the monk by the cowl
I know the master by the servant
I know the nun by the veil
I know when a hustler rattles on
I know fools raised on whipped cream
I know the wine by the barrel
I know everything but myself.
[. . .]

       —François Villon (1431–1463?), translated by Galway Kinnell

The Individual's Soliloquy
(excerpt)

I'm the individual.
First I lived by a rock
(I scratched some figures on it)
Then I looked for some place more suitable.
I'm the individual.
First I had to get myself food,
Hunt for fish, birds, hunt up wood
(I'd take care of the rest later)
Make a fire,
Wood, wood, where could I find any wood,
Some wood to start a little fire,
I'm the individual.
At the time I was asking myself,
Went to a canyon filled with air;

174

A voice answered me back:
I'm the individual.
So then I started moving to another rock,
I also scratched figures there,
Scratched out a river, buffaloes,
I'm the individual.
But I got bored with what I was doing,
Fire annoyed me,
I wanted to see more,
I'm the individual.
[. . .]

—Nicanor Parra (1914–), translated by Lawrence Ferlinghetti and Allen Ginsberg

Essay

I guess it's too late to live on the farm
I guess it's too late to move to a farm
I guess it's too late to start farming
I guess it's too late to begin farming
I guess we'll never have a farm
I guess we're too old to do farming
I guess we couldn't afford to buy a farm anyway
I guess we're not suited to being farmers
I guess we'll never have a farm now
I guess farming is not in the cards now
I guess Lewis wouldn't make a good farmer
I guess I can't expect we'll ever have a farm now
I guess I have to give up all my dreams of being a farmer
I guess I'll never be a farmer now
We couldn't get a farm anyway though Allen Ginsberg got one late in
      life
Maybe someday I'll have a big garden
I guess farming is really out
Feeding the pigs and the chickens, walking between miles of rows of
      crops
I guess farming is just too difficult
We'll never have a farm
Too much work and still to be poets
Who are the farmer poets
Was there ever a poet who had a self-sufficient farm

Flannery O'Connor raised peacocks
And Wendell Berry had a farm
Faulkner may have farmed a little
And Robert Frost had farmland
And someone told me Samuel Beckett farmed
Very few poets are real farmers
If William Carlos Williams could be a doctor and Charlie
    Vermont too,
Why not a poet who was also a farmer
Of course there was Brook Farm
And Virgil raised bees
Perhaps some poets of the past were overseers of farmers
I guess poets tend to live more momentarily
Than life on a farm would allow
You could never leave the farm to give a reading
Or go to a lecture by Emerson in Concord
I don't want to be a farmer but my mother was right
I should never have tried to rise out of the proletariat
Unless I can convince myself as Satan argues with Eve
That we are among a proletariat of poets of all the classes
Each ill-paid and surviving on nothing
Or on as little as one needs to survive
Steadfast as any farmer and fixed as the stars
Tenants of a vision we rent out endlessly
   —Bernadette Mayer (1945–)

All About Me

I am just a little guy
I really love a lot of trains
I have trains running through my veins
I got rhythm, I got soul
I got a grandma who's 85 years old
I am chubby
I am NOT ticklish
I am a great big muscular man
I try to work out as much as I can
I feel good
I am a Yankee Doodle Dandy
I love to ride horses
I hate tarantualas
I feel sick when I think of cauliflower

I jump on my parents' bed
I take no prisoners
I like to have a good laugh
I adore Japanese food
I hate to wear dresses
I am an artist of fashion
I wear a lot of stretch pants
I play office and teacher
I cry at weddings
I love black and white
I have an iguana
I wear braces
I like to play around
I do whatever I feel like
I have no known sicknesses
I am wicked but I don't show it
I am always nervous when I meet the dentist
I used to own a restaurant
I wish my name was Susie
I would like to be a writer
I hate Doctor Spock
I cry when I get squashed in a door
I can eat spinach day and night
I explore new candy stores
I have a gentle boyfriend
I am cool
I rode on a camel's hump
I dream about being an actor
I almost never frown
I try to cook but the food burns
I saw bats in Tennessee
I feel bad for some people
I hate peas
    —*Fifth grade class*

A corollary form is the *My* poem. "Sun and Water" by Martiniquan poet Aimé Césaire is an intriguing combination of simplicity and mysteriousness, like a collaboration between a kindergartner and a Surrealist. Students might want to write about the other three prime elements (My Air, My Earth, and My Fire), or about matters more personal (as Christopher Smart did when writing about his cat Jeoffrey).

Sun and Water

My water won't listen
my water sings like a secret
My water does not sing
my water rejoices like a secret
My water ferments
and rejoices through every reed
to the very milk of laughter
My water is a little child
my water is a deaf man
my water is a giant holding a lion to your chest
oh wine
vast immense
owing to the basilisk of your rich complicitous gaze
      —*Translated by Clayton Eshleman and Annette Smith*

He
(excerpt)

He cuts down the lakes so they appear straight
He smiles at his feet in their tired mules.
He turns up the music much louder.
He takes down the vaseline from the pantry shelf.

He is the capricious smile behind the colored bottles.
He eats not lest the poor want some.
He breathes of attitudes the piney altitudes.
He indeed is the White Cliffs of Dover.

He knows that his neck is frozen.
He snorts in the vale of dim wolves.
He writes to say, "If ever you visit this island,
He'll grow you back to your childhood.

"He is the liar behind the hedge
He grew one morning out of candor.
He is his own consolation prize.
He has had his eye on you from the beginning."
[. . .]
      —*John Ashbery (1927–)*

He

He is an agent
He is a dream
He is a copycat a little bit
He is fur
He is a girl-catcher
He is a playboy
He is a bat
He is a ghost
He is crazy because he'll break his leg leaping over tall buildings
He is from Mars
He is a beetle bug
He is good-looking
He is a monkey's uncle
He is a pest
He fights against Thrush
He's my man
He's in my shoes
He's got a telephone in his shoes
He's in my hair and he slides down my back
He's on a wheel
He sleeps in his gravel
He's a cute little thing
He has an ingrown toenail
He has a snoopy nose
He has fake hair
He lives in a secret hideout behind a shoemaker's shop
He gets dressed in a telephone booth
He's my Uncle
He wears secret weapons under his shoe
He loves me
He saved America
He saved my toenails
   —*Fourth to sixth grade group*

She
(excerpt)

[. . .]
She took two steps forward
She took two steps backward

179

The first step said good morning mister
The second step said good morning lady
And the other steps whispered how're the kids
This day's as lovely as a sky full of pigeons

She was wearing a burning brassiere
She had eyes rocked to sleep by the sea
She had buried her dreams in a windy closet
She had come on a dead man wedged in her head

When she got here one lovely part of her was still miles away
When she left something shot up on the skyline and waited for her
[. . .]
    —*Vicente Huidobro (1893–1948), translated by*
    Jerome Rothenberg

Brief Lives

These amusing capsule autobiographies in catalog verse are
distantly related to the "pronoun poems" above:

For a Dictionary

Philippe Soupault in his bed
born on a Monday
baptized on a Tuesday
married on a Wednesday
sick on a Thursday
dying on a Friday
dead on a Saturday
buried on a Sunday
That's the life of Philippe Soupault
    —*Philippe Soupault (1897–1990), translated by Ron Padgett*

If, After I Die

If, after I die, they should want to write my biography,
There's nothing simpler.
I've just two dates—of my birth, and of my death.
In between the one thing and the other all the days are mine.

I am easy to describe.
I lived like mad.
I loved things without any sentimentality.
I never had a desire I could not fulfill, because I never went blind.
Even hearing was to me never more than an accompaniment of seeing.
I understood that things are real and all different from each other;
I understood it with the eyes, never with thinking.
To understand it with thinking would be to find them all equal.

One day I felt sleepy like a child.
I closed my eyes and slept.
And by the way, I was the only Nature poet.
     —Fernando Pessoa (1888–1935), translated by Jonathan Griffin

Last Day on Earth

What would you do if you knew you had just twenty-four hours left to live? Some kids can figure it down to the last minute. One's own death seems like a remote concept to most children, so they react to this idea playfully, or at least not morbidly. There are even some details about wills and funeral arrangements, and speculations about the afterlife. Feel free to select and assemble the responses to this assignment, as I have done in the following poem.

If I Had 24 Hours Left to Live...

First I would go to the doctor and ask him if he could come up with
    a formula so I wouldn't die
Then I would play Lotto
I would spend one hour watching television and one hour studying
    science
I would pray to my mom who's passed away
I promised her that I want us to be side by side
My toys and clothes to my nieces
My jewelry will be buried with me
My coffin would be thick white glass
I would go to Coney Island and win a stuffed animal
I want them to play the song "All the Way to Heaven"
Just so there is no fighting I will leave my man-eating crocodile to Mr.
    Lipsitz
First we would go to McDonald's for lunch

Then we'd go swimming in an indoor pool
Then the girls would play the boys in basketball
After that, the men in the family would play the women in the family
And after that, we'd all play together
Later on in the day we'd play football
I would sock my cousin so hard he would think he'd made it to heaven
     before I did
I would draw the very perfect picture I never drew before
I would scare somebody and make them faint
I would break gravity in the middle of the earth and people would go
     into space
I would kill my little sister for all the bad things she did to me
I would celebrate over her death
I would like to be buried in a turquoise dress with pink and white trim
Pink and white shoes
I would change all my test scores on the computer to excellents and
     100s
I would change my will about giving Latisha 2¢
I would donate my body to science
Or have myself put in suspended animation
But I hope I will have an afterlife
And in that life I would get married and have lots of children
I would live in a mansion and have about ten maids and I would pay
     them evenly
I would give my niece my school supplies
After I die I want to be a sleeping beauty
I will want to be recreated again and go to heaven and work for God
And then come back and meet more people
And be an angel and a happy girl

I'd go to visit my old teacher Miss Loman
I'd buy a mink coat and I'd die in it
I'd go to a club
I'd keep putting on the hits
I'd make a big Blimpie sandwich
I'd tell them to bury me in a pyramid
I'd still have my glasses on
I would look at the stars for one last time
     —*Various fifth and sixth graders*

If I Had 24 Hours Left to Live

12:00 mid. Too tired to sleep, too awake to stay awake. I went
downstairs and then to Connecticut on my motorbike.

1:00 to 3:00 A.M. At the Ferrari dealer and bought a Ferrari Upfront 328 with my credit card, knowing that I wouldn't have to pay.

3:00 to 5:00. Speeding 150 mph alongside James Boone in a race back to New York.

5:00 to 7:00. Went to the car show and bought the Batmobile and drove home. Had to buy a chauffeur to drive the Ferrari.

7:00 to 1:00. Got off the plane to England. Still have the credit card.

1:00 to 3:00. Ask these nonspeaking English brats where the Lamborghini dealer is.

3:00. Bought a Lamborghini.

3:00 to 8:00. Out joyriding.

8:00 to 11:00. Sit around on my hands and knees mad at everything.

11:00 to midnight. I'm dying. They drive my Lamborghini. It's white. I sit in it.

Midnight. I feel the dirt hitting the exotic European masterpiece. I die.
 —*Peter Martinez, seventh grade*

The Snow Is Not Sticking

This poem is included as an example of a catalog poem that occured spontaneously. My third graders and I set out to write a cityscape poem. It had just begun to snow, so we tried to describe the snowfall using metaphor and simile. Someone mentioned the "first flakes" falling. According to third grade logic, there would be second and third flakes, and so on.

The Snow Is Not Sticking

The purple clouds burst in the air
Like a herd of smoky pillows
Angels are having a pillow fight

183

While the birds are playing hide and seek
The first flakes twinkle like aspirin and tumble down
The second flakes float to earth like tiny parachutes
The third flakes are like tiny parachutes
The fourth flakes are the ghosts of jellybeans
The fifth flakes whiz by like wads of onion paper
The sixth flakes fly like helium balloons
The seventh flakes pour like salt over the salad
The eighth flakes hop like rabbits in the Milky Way
The ninth flakes shiver like nervous eggs
The tenth flakes cover the bare branches of bushes in Flatbush
Houses are covered
Dirt is a white blanket
Heads, hats, shoulders, and shoes are buried in the heavenly sugar
But it's not sticking
Quietly it melts into little ribbons of water
Floating under the earth
    —Third grade group

Senses Plus

The simple idea here is to use the senses as a take-off point for a list poem. Each line would begin *I feel* (or *hear, see, taste, smell*). Ciamac Moallemi's poem below is an unusual example. When I tried this assignment in another school, other verbs began to sneak in and flavor the soup, so to speak.

I feel my limbs uniting on my body like a coterie of established friends
I hear questions the most adept philosopher could not answer
I see blackness like a dark abyss
I smell the air of insecurity and curiosity
I feel my brain being impregnated with knowledge
I hear answers from which more questions arise
I taste a fluid whose neutrality stuns me
I feel as if I lie in suspended animation
All of a sudden, I see the hands of a man in a white mask
I feel myself being pulled out of a passage
I see a room with a bunch of people around me
I feel creation
    —Ciamac Moallemi, eighth grade

Untitled Masterpiece

I understand the human heart
I wish the world was fixed
I try to stay away from trouble
I laugh at Benny Hill
I touch the whiskers on my father's face
I sleep in a freezing cold room
I sleep gracefully
I dream I could be a great teacher
I cry because I am touched
I touch an unknown thing when my curiosity wanders inside me
I hear the city rumble
I smell the Botanical Gardens
I touch my head when I see a nut!
I taste the medicine of accidents
I imagine a new word in my dreams
I pretend to be the man of the house when my father's gone
I feel happy, sad, whatever the time calls for, good, bad, whatever is
    right
I pretend to be what I want most and then let my mind relax
I smell pie from miles away
I know my mother's going to have a baby
I wish you would stop peeking at my paper
I say my thoughts openly
I taste a sour, bitter world
I hear a beautiful sound—still and silent
I smell an odor of accomplishment
I see and I remember
I know I am myself
I wonder why I'm here today
I dream of snow-covered mountains and gurgling streams
I wonder what I would do without you
You pretend to care for me but there's really someone else
I understand that I can't love you like once before
I wonder what would happen if I ever lost that loving
I wonder why I wonder
I feel this wall separating our love
I try to overcome this fear of loneliness but it's almost impossible
I hope for a brand new world and endless summer
I enjoy small talk and big lies of memories shared by forever friends
I wish I could speak a little more Japanese

I feel a mink coat rub against my arms
I hear beautiful music and the ranchers calling cattle in Texas
I wish I was in Dixie, hooray!
I pretend sometimes I'm Queen of the Fish
I say weird things people don't understand
I understand you have a slight problem in the back seat
I imagine a big giant pink thing when I sleep
I hope Bob Hope will come to my house
I smell the ink on the test papers
I love the night life at times when I am alone
I think about animals, rocks, and shells
I see the fog in Manhattan and . . .
I smell the horrible smell of it
I wonder if I'll ever get married
I know I'm crazy because my pop is
I feel like a lord because I'm strong
I see myself in the mirror
I smell like a bar of Coast soap
I touch everything in sight
I like my dog because he bites people
I cry when I get belted because I'm bad
I make models because they're cool
I think I'm going to run away
I have a nasty brother because he is no good
I don't hit girls because they're not boys
I could go out and hang out
I want to be married because I can't wait
I wonder about myself
I have to go to Abraham and Straus
I know 8,417 words with an f
I wonder what my mom is doing when she tells me not to go in the
    kitchen
I understand my sister's problems
I like to eat soup with a fork because I don't like soup
I don't like fish, liver, or strawberry ice cream
I taste the great taste of margarine
I need some blankets to warm me up
I understand what you mean, it happened to me too
I smell like a rose some people say
I dream like a cat
I feel like a pretzel that is crying
I wonder if I can love a dream

I know Mr. Fagin is a dragon
I see Mr. Fagin's tootsie roll body
I touch a lion with a feather
I try to be needed
I don't have a toad
I want to get married to Catherine Beach
I understand monkey business
I try to do my best in a swimming pool
I wonder if the '50s will come back
I laugh when my cousin blows up his frogs
I wish Laura Ingalls Wilder were still alive
I understand that life is work
I know that people are just like children
I imagine our play will be a success
I feel like a wondrous poet!
I say, "Watson, let's go for a walk!"
I dream of a teacher without a brain
I sleep through a purple thunderstorm
I enjoy the flowers of the forest
I play with the idea of love
I fight against the devil who is trying to possess me
I love chocolate pudding
I hear my mother calling me
    —*Fourth and fifth grade group*

Compare this catalog to Whitman's "Song of Myself" and the "I" entries in indexes of first lines in poetry anthologies.

Insults

There are precedents in poetry and song for this type of catalog, most notably in Islamic culture and the African-American tradition of "The Dozens"—a good-natured trading of clever put-downs. I suggest that if the good nature can't be maintained as the keynote of this activity, forget it.

Insults

You're a bum
You're a hypochondriac

You don't meditate, you just say things
You don't know how to make a speech
You're going to stand on your head and spit nickels in the afternoon
Your head is like a watermelon
Your head is like a ski slope
You're a walking broomstick
Your mother wears army boots
No wonder you started to make pancakes—someone flattened your
     head
Why do you have bad breath when you can't afford any onions?
Your breath is so bad that when you say "Hi" it's like a hurricane
You can't afford a phone so you talk into a shoe
You look like a monkey with glasses on
Your feet stink
Your arms are like french fries
You need Scope mouthwash
When you shave you break the razor
You have a lot of dandruff in your mustache
It breaks the scissors
Your dandruff is as big as bowling balls
You're so dirty you can plant radishes in your hair
And potatoes in your ears
Your hair smells like a dozen zoos
How bad can you get
You're so old-fashioned you're rooting for Popeye
Your sneeze is so loud that all the planets explode
Your teeth are like Swiss cheese
Shut up and sit down and don't touch the merchandise
You big baby
Your mother looks like Charlie Brown
Your Adam's apple is growing a mustache
Last time you went to play pool, when you shot the 8 ball it got hair
     all over it
You speak the truth with false teeth
You look like a dried-out rat
Your pants have 3 lbs. of starch in them
Your head has only one strand of hair
Your mouth is like a chicken's beak
Your neck is as long as a stork
Your head is like a starfish
Your feet are like ape feet
Your nose is like a banana

Your eyes are 1,000 inches long
You got 20 lbs. of grease on your face
Your tie has holes with bugs living in them
Larry's the fat man in the circus
Your breath is bad enough to crack a wall
Mr. Rosenbloom's hair is as long as The Beatles'
Your mother drinks ammonia
Your mother's mustache
Your mother wears pointed house slippers
You've got ingrown bedbugs
I walked in your house and stepped on a cigarette and your mother said,
   "Who turned out the lights?"
   —*Various fifth and sixth graders*

The Third Eye

Having a third eye that can see what the other two eyes can't is
an appealing idea to most children, the satisfying fantasy of being
omniscient. Poet Ron Padgett invented this writing idea.

With My Third Eye

I can see the moon with spacemen
I can see the sun in space
I can see Casper the Ghost in a haunted house
I can see Martians, the Wizard of Oz, Grape Ape
I can see red and white witches in a brown and blue candy house
I can see God in heaven and inside everybody
I can see 8 miles from here
I can see all 50 states
I can see Larry Fagin in his house on the moon
I can see a tyrannosaurus in the forest
I can see Santa Claus making toys in his lab on the North Pole
I can see Wonder Woman in Washington, D.C.
I can make a rocket go up without launching it
I can do homework in a fingersnap
I can make the TV fly
   —*Second grade group*

My Third Eye

My third eye can see the good in bad people.
My third eye can see me in my mother's stomach.
My third eye can see me in my coffin and in heaven, I hope.
My third eye can see the destruction and beginning of the earth and
    universe.
My third eye can see the death of the world from the energy crisis.
My third eye can see me trading my wife for a blond.
    —*Tim Eldridge, fifth grade*

The Divergent List Poem

Traditionally a list in a poem bears a direct and understandable relation to that poem. Contemporary poet Susan Timmons's "Poem" doesn't do that. In it, her list of British writers and the rest of the text seem to veer away from each other. The reader is tempted to fill the gap by imagining a connection between the two parts:

Poem

cause I want crinkled foil and water
CHAUCER and rose petals, are additionally desirable
SHAKESPEARE   and also able to look over at
SPENSER   shadows on lawn of
MILTON   stately Arkansas statehood.
BLAKE
KEATS

SWIFT

Some students will be permanently perplexed by this poem, but others will enjoy its inspired battiness and will want to try writing divergent list poems of their own.

Math Poems

Even mathematics is a fit subject for list poetry. Carl Sandburg instructs and advises in this whimsical poem:

Arithmetic

Arithmetic is where numbers fly like pigeons in and out of your head.

Arithmetic tells you how many you lose or win if you know how many you had before you lost or won.

Arithmetic is seven times eleven all good children go to heaven—or five six bundles of sticks.

Arithmetic is numbers you squeeze from your head to your hand to your pencil to your paper till you get the answer.

Arithmetic is where the answer is right and everything is nice and you can look out the window and see the blue sky—or the answer is wrong and you have to start all over and have to see how it comes out this time.

If you take a number and double it and double it again and then double it a few more times, the number gets bigger and goes higher and higher and only arithmetic can tell you what the number is when you decide to quit doubling.

Arithmetic is where you have to multiply—and you carry the multiplication table in your head and hope you won't lose it.

If you have two small animal crackers, one good and one bad, and you eat one, and a striped zebra with streaks all over him eats the other, how many animal crackers will you have if somebody offers you five six seven and you say No no no and you say Nay nay nay and you say Nix nix nix?

If you ask your mother for one fried egg for breakfast and she gives you two fried eggs and you eat both of them, who is better in arithmetic, you or your mother?

The following twelfth graders add a personal slant to geometry:

Geometry & Life

There is a place
with lines I call
my paper. There
are circles made

191

out of holes. The
corners are hyperbolas
with no pairs to
match. My pencil
makes an axis
going z. My focus
is at this point,
which is dimensionless.
But now I'll stop
before I reach infinity.
        —*Brenda Keene, twelfth grade*

The Way Geometry Affects My Life

Parabola
carlights
Hyperbola
satellites
Circle
tires
Sphere
earth
Ellipse
football
Point
place on earth
Line
road
Vortex
bottom of a bowl where the marble rests
Square
block
Triangle
trusses
Infinity
never ending
Asymptote
never-crossing paths
Origin
back to the beginning
        —*Mike Edwards, twelfth grade*

Practically Geometry

a river on a map of an ocean
quantum physics and organic compounds
letters
derive an ellipse equation
parabolic baseball home run
the curve of a cloud
an airplane wing's shape
a bird's feather shape
equations, pi, and conic section
an Ivy League school
satellite TV dishes and MTV
planet rotation
and mindless faces gazing at the teacher, spaced out.
　　　—*Michael Smith, twelfth grade*

Hodgepodge

The following poems require no commentary.

If They Could Talk, What Would They Say?

Coffee pot: I'm burning my bottom!
Clock: My hands can change numbers.
Skeleton: My back is killing me.
Chair: Fat people stay off me!
Sun: Please don't come out, Mr. Moon!
Mirror: Take the baby off me!
Sun: I'm so hot I could blow up the earth!
　　　—*Second grade group*

Ten Things I'll Need on a Desert Island

Food (ravioli, Beefaroni, etc.)
Clothes (thick pants, heavy sweater, pajamas, socks)
Drink (grape juice, cherry juice, water, etc.)
Bug spray
A book to improve my reading
Silverware (I can't eat with my hands!)
Checkered coat

Tay-lord pants
Filmstrip and projector
Cushion
Some knives
A small furry toy for company
A watch with the date on it
Fishing rod
Spear
Ax
Shoes so my feet do not burn
A fold-up electric wheelchair
Nails
Girls
Car seat for a baby
A whole set of bricks to build a school with 10,300 calendars
A bowl to eat my cereal
Model car
Spirograph game
Little pieces of wood
Napkins and tissues
A puzzle to make
A puppet to talk to
Erasers
Violins
Pom poms
Barbie dolls
My teacher
    —Various fourth and fifth graders

Christmas Presents I Would Give

My brother a foot on his head
My mother a watch that says peekaboo
My uncle an elephant shirt
My sister a double sink
My father eyeballs
Grandma a punch in the nose
Grandpa a tidal wave
My cousin a can of monkey polish
My little dog a red rose
My cat a bottle of Avon perfume
James Brown another Afro

Aretha Franklin a glass hatchet
Sammy Davis, Jr., a typewriter
Jerry Lewis some songs to copyright
Dean Martin a needle (in his behind)
Ray Charles a wooden fox
Agnew 7,000 bullets in his back
Humphrey a hump
Nixon $1,000
Batman an ant
Robin a germ
Superman a grand piano
Diana Ross a ticket to God
The Flintstones a window
Santa Claus a glass of warm water
    —*Fourth grade group*

Fear

I am afraid of being trapped in an umbrella
I am afraid of ice balls in my eyes
I am afraid of report card day
Of being left back
Of splitting my pants
Losing my friends
Of my dog being locked in the bathroom
Of walking in the South Bronx
Of returning to school after summer vacation
Of meeting my grandfather who I never saw before
Of not understanding a new explanation
Of lying on a bed of nails
Losing my parents
Seeing my name on a tombstone
Looking at a corpse
Losing my little sister in a supermarket
Being on "Candid Camera"
Falling off a cliff
Bumping into a fruit stand
I am afraid of the school hot lunch
Afraid of having an allergy to water
    —*Fifth grade group*

Childhood Emergencies

My mother had to exercise my feet because they were crippled
I used to swallow air; my mother had to squeeze me
I broke my mother's glass coffee table and had to have stitches in my
    head
I was born with a short arm
I went to Bermuda
I saw the Grand Canyon
I licked a battery and almost died
I fell in a big hole
I got a shock from an iron plug
I almost drowned in the bathtub
I banged my head and saw an empty red boot walking up the hall
I sat in glass
My brother locked me up in a suitcase; it was foggy
I fell out of my crib and my heart stopped beating
I bumped into a dresser and had seven stitches
The stove blew up and burned the side of my face
I drank Clorox from the bottle and my eyes were glassy
I put my hands through a glass door
The week after I was born I couldn't breathe and didn't have a name;
    they called me Rungnatee which means "born in the morning"
I was hit by a car; it tickled
My legs were hanging out the window; I almost fell
I ran into a wall and got this knot that way
I got hit in the stomach by a swing
I fainted (dropped out) when Clifton was born; he was blue
I saw a tractor take off my father's leg
I saw a train run over a boy's toe
    —*Fourth grade group*

Birthday Sonnet

I've never used the following list poem by Edwin Denby as an
example for writing. It just seemed like a nice way to end this book.

A Postcard

Elaine, Nini, Sylvia, Marjorie, Theda,
Each sends you happy wishes for your birthday,

Red and black Frances, Frannie, and Almavida,
Louise, gay Germaine too who is far away,
Kind Maggie, and Pit, Martha who prays gladly,
Jeannie, Ruth, Ernestine, Anne, Billie Holiday,
Husky Patsy, Ilse they love so madly,
And straighforward Teddy—Dear Rudy, they all say.
And then Victor, and Bill, and Walter the mild,
And Frank, David, John, Aaron, Paul, Harry and
Virgil, the Photoleague, Oliver, Ebbie wild,
I and Gankie and the Shoe-man shake your hand.
Marieli and Susan come running at the end
And all of us send our love to you, our friend.

Select Bibliography
Books, Magazines, and Records

Allison, Alexander W., et al., eds. *The Norton Anthology of Poetry*. New York: Norton, 1975. Includes the Earl of Surrey's poem "The Happy Life" as "My Friend, the Things That Do Attain."

Ashbery, John. *Rivers and Mountains*. New York: Ecco Press, 1977.

_____. *Some Trees*. New Haven, Ct.: Yale University Press, 1956.

Ashbery, John, et al., eds. *Locus Solus*, no. 2. Lans-en-Vercors, France: 1961

Astrov, Margot, ed. *American Indian Prose and Poetry*. New York: Capricorn Books, 1962.

Berrigan, Ted. *So Going around Cities*. Berkeley, Ca.: Blue Wind Press, 1980.

Brainard, Joe. *I Remember*. New York: Full Court Press, 1975.

Césaire, Aimé. *The Collected Poetry of Aimé Césaire*. Berkeley, Ca.: University of California Press, 1983. Trans. Clayton Eshleman and Annette Smith.

Cheever, John. *The Stories of John Cheever*. New York: Alfred A. Knopf, 1978.

Cole, Michael and Roy D'Andrade. "The Influence of Schooling on Concept Formation: Some Preliminary Conclusions." *The Quarterly Newsletter of the Laboratory of Comparative Cognition*, no. 4 (April 1984).

Collom, Jack. *Moving Windows: Evaluating the Poetry Children Write*. New York: Teachers & Writers Collaborative, 1985.

Denby, Edwin. *Complete Poems*. New York: Random House, 1986.

Derricotte, Toi and Madeline Tiger. *Creative Writing: A Manual for Teachers*. Trenton, N.J.: New Jersey State Council on the Arts, n.d.

Ginsberg, Allen. *Collected Poems 1947–1980*. New York: Harper & Row, 1984.

Goody, Jack. *The Domestication of the Savage Mind*. Cambridge, England: Cambridge University Press, 1977.

Grossman, Florence. *Getting from Here to There: Writing and Reading Poetry*. Montclair, N.J.: Boynton/Cook, 1982.

Hansen, Jane, Thomas Newkirk, and Donald Graves. *Breaking Ground: Teachers Relate Reading and Writing in the Elementary School*. Portsmouth, N.H.: Heinemann, 1985.

Huidobro, Vicente. *The Selected Poetry of Vicente Huidobro*. New York: New Directions, 1981. Ed. David Guss.

Jarrell, Randall. *Poetry and the Age*. New York: Octagon, 1972.

Jason, Philip K. and Allan B. Lefkowitz. *Creative Writer's Handbook*. Englewood Cliffs, N.J.: Prentice Hall, 1990.

Kenner, Hugh. *Seventeenth-Century Poetry*. San Francisco: Rinehart Press, 1964. Includes Herrick's "Argument of His Book" and Lord Cherbery's "A Description."

Kerouac, Jack. *Lonesome Traveler*. New York: Grove, 1960.

Koch, Kenneth. *The Pleasures of Peace*. New York: Grove, 1969.

_____. *Wishes, Lies and Dreams: Teaching Children to Write Poetry*. New York: Harper & Row, 1970.

Koch, Kenneth and Kate Farrell. *Talking to the Sun: An Illustrated Anthology of Poems for Young People*. New York: The Metropolitan Museum of Art and Holt, Rinehart and Winston, 1985.

Larbaud, Valery. *The Poems of A. O. Barnabooth*. Tokyo: Mushinsha Ltd., 1977. Trans. Ron Padgett and Bill Zavatsky.

Mayer, Bernadette. *The Golden Book of Words*. New York: Angel Hair Books, 1978.

Myers, Jack and Michael Simms, eds. *The Longman Dictionary and Handbook of Poetry*. New York: Longman, 1985.

North, Charles. *Leap Year: Poems 1968–78*. New York: Kulchur Foundation, 1978.

Padgett, Ron, ed. *The Teachers & Writers Handbook of Poetic Forms*. New York: Teachers & Writers Collaborative, 1987.

Pessoa, Fernando. *Selected Poems*. Harmondsworth, England: Penguin Books, 1974. Trans. Jonathan Griffin.

Picard, Max. *The World of Silence*. Washington, D.C.: Regnery Gateway, 1988.

Preminger, Alex, ed. *The Princeton Encyclopedia of Poetry and Poetics*. Princeton, N.J.: Princeton University Press, 1974.

Rabelais, François. *Gargantua and Pantegruel*. New York: Norton, 1990. Trans. Burton Raffel.

Sandburg, Carl. *Harvest Poems 1910–1960*. San Diego: Harcourt Brace Jovanovich, 1960.

Shapiro, David. *Lateness*. Woodstock, N.Y.: Overlook Press, 1977.

Shonagon, Sei. *The Pillow Book of Sei Shonagon*. Harmondsworth, England: Penguin Books, 1976. Trans. Ivan Morris.

Smart, Christopher. *Jubilate Agno*. New York: Greenwood Press, 1969. The cat Jeoffrey selection is also available in many anthologies.

Snyder, Gary. *Three Worlds. Three Realms. Six Roads*. Marlboro, Vt.: Griffin Press, 1968.

Thomas, Henry. *Complete Recorded Works*. Glen Cove, N. Y.: Herwin Records, 1974.

Timmons, Susan. *Locked from the Outside*. Chicago: Yellow Press, 1990.

Villon, François. *The Poems of François Villon*. Boston: Houghton Mifflin, 1977. Trans. Galway Kinnell.

Waldman, Anne. *Baby Breakdown*. New York: Bobbs-Merrill, 1970.

_____. *Fast Speaking Woman*. San Francisco: City Lights Books, 1975.

Whalen, Philip. *On Bear's Head*. New York: Harcourt, Brace & World, Inc. and Coyote, 1969.

Whitman, Walt. *Leaves of Grass*. New York: Norton, 1965.

Ziegler, Alan. *The Writing Workshop: Vol. 2*. New York: Teachers & Writers Collaborative, 1984.